The Manager's Short Course

BIL and CHER HOLTON

John Wiley & Sons, Inc.
New York, Chichester, Brisbane, Toronto, Singapore

To those managers
who have guts enough
to transfer training to the real world

Library of Congress Cataloging-in-Publication Data

Holton, Bil. 1947–
    The manager's short course / by Bil and Cher Holton.
      p. cm.
    Includes bibliographical references.
    ISBN 0-471-55166-X (cloth).—ISBN 0-471-55167-8 (paper)
    1. Career development.   I. Holton, Cher, 1950– . II. Title.
HF5549.5.C35H65   1992
658.4'09—dc20   91-22840

Printed in the United States of America

10 9 8 7 6 5 4 3 2 1

Printed and bound by Courier Companies, Inc.

Foreword

As we approach the close of the twentieth century, a revolution in education is in the making. Some signs of the impending revolution are visible in elementary and secondary education, more in higher education, but most of the changes are happening in adult education/training/human resources development. And this book is on the moving edge of that revolution.

This revolution is beginning now rather than earlier or later for several reasons. The aging of our population is one; with the shrinking proportion of children and youth and the growing proportion of adults, the focus of our educational efforts must shift from the young to the mature. The accelerating pace of change—the knowledge explosion and technological revolution—is another; the shortening time span of human obsolescence, especially in the world of work, is requiring us to conceive of learning as a lifelong process and to provide resources for a continuous program of self-renewal. The shift in educational research from a focus on teaching to a focus on learning is a third reason, and the resultant explosion of knowledge about how learning takes place is causing us to reorganize our way of thinking away from strategies for providing episodic instruction to strategies for engaging human beings in a process of day-in, day-out, self-directed learning, with the help of facilitators and resource people who are all around them (if they know how to find them).

One of the special virtues of this book, in my estimation, is that it is andragogical all the way. It faithfully but imaginatively applies the most up-to-date concepts and principles of adult education. It calls for involving managers actively in planning and carrying out their self-development projects. It calls for respecting their experience and making use of it as a resource for learning. It shows how learning experiences can be organized around real-life situations and result in improvement in the performance of real-life tasks. It is highly practical, but theoretically sound.

Most important, it is just plain fun to read.

Malcolm S. Knowles

Preface

In our travels around this great country of ours, in settings as distant geographically and culturally as a North Carolina tele-communications headquarters, a snow-covered heavy truck manufacturer in Utah, an Ohio electronics firm nestled in the stuffy air of a large metropolitan area, a national association's convention in the suffocating smog of Los Angeles, and an im-maculate electronics manufacturing plant in Florida's humidity, we have been struck by many a manager's full-throated cry to provide legitimate alternatives to costly classroom training—alternatives that would transfer training to the real world.

We hear a renewed recognition of the importance of ensur-ing that management training programs provide the kind of lead-ership development experiences that lend themselves to honest and practical skills acquisition. Unfortunately, no matter how well simulated or reality-based it is, classroom training is noth-ing more than *preparing to do.* Ask any professional athlete in any sport, in any league, the difference between practice and a nationally telecast championship game. Michael Jordan says about 25 percent. (His field goal percentage in practice is 78 percent—in a game it's generally 45–53 percent.) Tom Peters, author of *Thriving on Chaos,* says the best way to improve one's platform speaking skills is to increase the number of *at bats.* You can devote a considerable number of hours to practicing for the speech and speak perfectly. Standing before an expectant audi-ence of more than a thousand people can produce sweaty palms, nervousness, and forgotten lines. All the aerial combat training in the world—no matter how sophisticated, precise, rigorous, or authentic—will not *guarantee* battle performance. Only the stench and heat of battle will validate how much of the training gets transferred to the trigger-finger accuracy and aerial show-manship of a confident and battle-savvy ace.

Training for meaningful results demands doing the right things. Classroom training is part of the right stuff. In-the-trenches applicability is where classroom training meets the real world. The call is for experiential alternatives to classroom training so that well-trained alumni can pull motivational triggers skillfully and lead colleagues proudly and productively through corporate battlefields.

The extraordinary demands of today's marketplace make it mandatory for organizations to offer development options that include a full range of self-management skills. When targeted development is designed to enhance both job performance and personal growth (inside and outside of traditional classroom experiences), the developmental scaffolding is complete. Therefore, we subscribe to the self-directed learning approach developed by Malcolm Knowles, professor emeritus at North Carolina State University. In its broadest meaning *self-directed learning* is the process of self-managed development whereby individuals use available resources (human and material) to achieve identified learning outcomes. It demands initiative and self-discipline on the part of the learner, who must assume a proactive role in setting goals, identifying resources, selecting and implementing appropriate learning strategies, and evaluating performance improvement outcomes.

As human potential consultants, we recognize the use of a wide variety of targeted development strategies to foster high potential management growth. The four major sources that constitute the developmental matrix subscribed to by our firm are Selected Work Experiences, Personal Development Experiences, Internal Industry-Specific Programs, and College and University Programs.

This systems approach to managerial development legitimizes the developmental mix between personal and professional education. Both are necessary ingredients in well-planned and well-timed executive development.

Many organizations have formal industry-specific leadership development programs in place. The availability of college and university programs in most cities offers human resource departments a wide range of general management and technical training opportunities. However, these two options are only half of the developmental pie. So often limited time and resources prevent organizations from taking full advantage of these classroom-intensive resources. Other kinds of developmental options must be explored to complement existing programs.

The focus of this book is to offer organizations 101 ways to bypass classroom training and still develop leadership skills for high-potential executives and managers. Why sidestep traditional training? Because

- The management principles we have held dear for one hundred years are undergoing relentless attack—and succumbing!
- In order to adapt to tomorrow's accelerated pace of change, managers are forced to challenge conventional wisdom at every turn.
- Managers must innovate constantly, or stagnate.
- Living with paradox and uncertainty demands clear vision, continuous risk-testing, stretching, adapting, and bias for action.
- Empowering people to outperform themselves means taking responsibility to enhance managerial skills each and every day.
- Managers can't attend formal training programs every day, so there has to be some other avenue for legitimate personal and professional development.

This book is one response to that need, and that's the Holton advantage . . . providing legitimate alternatives for sustained leadership development by helping ordinary people achieve extraordinary results.

This comprehensive book was written with some very specific people in mind:

- executives who want to invest in their own development and refine their managerial skills
- line managers and supervisors who need not only to develop themselves, but also to focus on the development of their employees, preparing them to take on greater responsibility and accountability
- supervisors who must function in a team-focused environ-

ment and are challenged to empower their employees to achieve phenomenal results
- fast-trackers who need to accelerate the acquisition of leadership skills
- employees who have career plans that include leadership positions
- human resource staff members who must stretch training dollars and identify viable alternative sources to the more traditional classroom training
- any individual who is looking for practical strategies to achieve phenomenal improvement in his or her leadership skills

The book is divided into eight major developmental areas that are critical for leadership success. Each area is a learning laboratory in itself, and includes performance improvement strategies that provide a daily dose of reality for the user. The eight categories include

- *Empowering People:* The prescriptions in this area help managers build a work environment that features a climate of trust, unfailing commitment, and integrity as bone-deep beliefs. It will provide the ongoing developmental mechanism managers need to help ordinary people achieve extraordinary results.
- *Modeling Leadership Excellence:* This area is designed to help managers develop that special dimension that separates leaders from the rest of the crowd. It provides specific strategies designed to clarify goals, build knowledge bases, and apply leadership skills in the trenches— creating the total leadership package.
- *Welcoming Change:* Managers must learn to welcome change as vigorously as they fought it in the past. These toe-in-the-water prescriptions are designed to help managers feel more comfortable in dealing with change.
- *Communicating for Results:* Enhancing each manager's repertoire of interpersonal communication skills is the aim of this section. It is packed with practical tactics that complement classroom training by providing real world opportunities to practice a variety of communication skills.

- *Managing Time:* Each of the strategies included in this area goes beyond superficial time management courses and zeroes in on specific time robbers. By using these prescriptions, conscientious managers can be bashers of time barriers and gain greater control over the quality of work life.
- *Customer Responsiveness:* These prescriptions provide practical strategies to help managers build a highly responsive service system, appreciate the distinction between internal and external customers, and reap well-deserved dividends in terms of profitability and customer loyalty.
- *Self-Mastery:* Based on the philosophy that whatever you conceive and believe, you can achieve, these prescriptions help motivate managers to reach their fullest potential both personally and professionally.
- *Targeted Innovation:* This area focuses on the idea that creative breakthroughs are lucrative, repeatable, and reliable economic events that can be expertly managed and reasonably predicted. Creativity is a learned skill—and this section gives managers the tools to tap that creative genius within themselves, their people, and their customers.

We unashamedly take pride in designing long-term leadership development systems geared to enhance a manager's credibility and confidence during his or her on-line activities. We have long believed that leadership development is a line function. Leaders are built on the firing line, in the trenches, out in the shops, eyeball to eyeball with customers and the troops.

Incrementalized learning is the key to sustained development. Executive skill development must be assigned a high-priority status. As human resource development consultants, we have always felt the need to ensure transfer of learning. Classroom training and formal development experiences have their place in the overall scope of management development. These types of experiences are excellent launch sites for the evolving manager. They establish trajectory and direction. Many provide conceptual parameters. Some motivate and stimulate. Others simply validate what is already known. To complement these big bang events, we proudly introduce 101 ways to bypass them for fun and profit. We see all these ways as lucrative, repeatable, and reliable "developmental snapshots" that will bring you portrait-quality managers, suitable for leading people confidently and expertly through the immense challenges ahead.

Special thanks and appreciation are due to the many managers and human resource development professionals who, through the years, gave us the practical insights that constitute a large portion of what this book has to offer. Manuscript preparation was particularly time-consuming and painstakingly rigorous, as it went through a number of drafts. Particularly meritorious contributors in editing, reediting, and word processing go to Nancy Whitaker, who gave generously of her time. Her dedication was heroic. Her patience extraordinary. Her singular support Herculean. The artwork of Ted Williams is delightful and adds just the right amount of play to introduce each chapter.

Contents

SECTION TWO

Modeling Leadership Excellence

SECTION THREE

Welcoming Change

SECTION FOUR

Communicating for Results

SECTION FIVE

Managing Time

The EXHIBITS*

* Corresponding prescription numbers appear within parentheses.

Management Skills and Related Prescription Inventory   223

Introduction

The path we recommend toward leadership excellence provides 101 ways to bypass formal classroom training. The road to success is through self-directed managerial development. Some routes will be rocky, strewn with challenges at every turn. Others will be a bit smoother, depending on the evolving manager's current level of skills and experience. All will take managers into the corporate trenches. Each will place managers—young and old, experienced and inexperienced, college prepared and streetwise—squarely on the firing line. Many of these truly enlightening prescriptions will propel the bravest of them headlong into the bowels of organizational realities.

Formal classroom training, although necessary and worthwhile, has never (and will never) provide the kind of reality testing that the evolving manager needs to make it in the real world. Practice—even perfect practice—can only position the learner to perform according to plan just in case the desired performance is needed in the real world. Preparation prepares the mind, not the heart. True development takes place when experience meets the road. Road-testing performance is what this book is all about.

There is compelling evidence that managers who take the initiative in developing leadership skills learn more in less time, enter into organizational experiences more purposefully, feel more empowered, develop more confidence earlier, and enjoy a more enriched and productive managerial experience than managers who only attend mountaintop classroom training experiences and sit passively at the feet of content gurus. Make no mistake about it: Both classroom and practical application experiences are critical ingredients in the total developmental loop. Both are necessary, but not sufficient.

Self-directed learning is the applications piece so vital for sustained improvement. It means taking personal responsibility for operationalizing targeted development. It means learning one step (sometimes a giant one) at a time. It means taking incremental leaps of faith. It calls for hammering out small wins. Risking failure. Putting one's professional credibility on the line. Sweating. Doubting. Adapting to relentless contingencies brought about by strobelike change. It also means winning. Achieving incredible results. Accepting praise. Cultivating leadership excellence eyeball to eyeball with customers and co-workers alike. It means standing taller. Walking with a distinct bounce in each step. And wearing a smile that just won't quit.

The simple truth is that no longer is it realistic (or even sane) to define the purpose of managerial development as transmitting what is known. The half-life of *facts* in today's marketplace of rapidly accelerating change is approaching the life span of a common housefly. What works today may not work next year— or even next week. The same strategy today may even *bury* a fragile business tomorrow. Thus the main purpose of managerial development must be to provide a supportive learning environment in which evolving leaders learn the skills of inquiry and survival. This parenting of the educational mix (learning-application-learning—) is the responsibility of each and every organization that expects to take its service or product to market. Avoiding this responsibility is the same thing as planned obsolescence. We're absolutely convinced of this. Unfailingly so.

What do we mean by self-directed learning? The best definition, by the concept's founder, Professor Emeritus Malcolm S. Knowles at North Carolina State University, will serve to lay the foundation for self-directed managerial development:

> In its broadest meaning, "self-directed learning" describes a process in which individuals take the initiative, with or without the help of others, in diagnosing their learning needs, formulating learning goals, identifying human and material resources for learning, choosing and implementing appropriate learning strategies, and evaluating learning outcomes. Other labels found in the literature to describe this process are "self-planned learning," "self-instruction," "self-teaching," "self-study," and "autonomous learning." The trouble with most of these labels is that they seem to imply learning in isolation, whereas self-directed learning usually takes place in association with various kinds of helpers, such as teachers, tutors, mentors, resource people, and peers. There is a lot of mutuality among a group of self-directed learners.
>
> Knowles, M. S., *Self-Directed Learning*, Chicago: Follett Publishing Co., 1975.

The partnership between student and teacher, organization and evolving manager, leader and follower must be real and close-knit. Constant and open communication is critical to its success. Continuous reciprocation of what is learned is paramount for sustained and lasting skills development. The climate for learning must be one of unfailing trust, unwavering faith, and unmitigated commitment. To be effective, the transmitting of knowledge will *have* to go *both ways*—from organization to evolving manager and from evolving manager to organization. The coaches, mentors, and sponsors assigned to educate the evolving manager will themselves be educated by the growing awareness and experience of the evolving leader. Total receptivity to mistakes, failures, eye-opening insights, change, the uncovering of obsolete rules or policies, the amount of patience it takes to gain competence in a new skill, new and innovative thinking, and attempts to challenge tradition must be guaranteed and unconditional. The days of cop and referee are over.

We believe many of the mistakes that managers make with people and task accomplishment stem from preoccupation with the impending doom associated with a wrong move or honest failure. Mistakes and misfires are generally punished. Relentless pressure is applied. No wonder managers hesitate to apply what is learned in formal classroom settings. To practice new skill acquisitions (error-free) in the corporate trenches often means martyrdom if the newly acquired skill isn't perfectly executed. Unless the organization is willing enough and patient enough to provide a climate conducive to the growing pains associated with learning, leadership excellence will be nothing more than a pipe dream.

To use a sports analogy, if your Pro-Bowl quarterback tosses an interception in a divisional play-off game during the first series of downs, the worst thing the coach can do is to bench him. When the defense prevents its opponent from making a first down (forcing them to punt), the organization that wants to develop a brilliant young quarterback will encourage him to get back in there and pass the ball again. The offensive line coach will review quickly how what went wrong went wrong. Teammates offer encouragement. The front office may even telephone to offer support. Leadership development in the marketplace is no different. Misfires from evolving managers must not only be tolerated, but also welcomed with open arms. Coaching must occur immediately. Inquisitions, hangings, and firing squads eliminated.

Unless organizations adopt an honest, unshakable belief that big bang classroom training experiences are only launching pads for on-the-job, self-directed developmental learning projects, the money spent on training might as well be flushed down corporate toilets. Please reread that sentence aloud and with conviction. Now put your right palm over your right ear and read the first sentence aloud one more time. The reason we ask you to cover your ear is that what you have just read is so vital for ensuring sustained managerial development that we didn't want it to go into one ear— and out the other! You know as well as we do that unless learning is applied—and targeted—it has little use. Corporate dollars are hard-won in today's marketplace. It makes good sense to ensure a proper return on investment. Each of the 101 prescriptions outlined in this book is a self-directed learning laboratory—stretching your training dollars, multiplying your human resource dividends.

A comparison between traditional classroom education and self-directed learning will help crystallize the differences and complementary nature of the two learning technologies:

Classroom Education

- Evolving managers are essentially dependent on what information is provided by the consultant or trainer according to the lesson plan. All participants receive the same basic information.

- Knowledge is transmitted from gurus to participants. Written materials and course aids are basically generic. Participants' experiences tend to be seen as less valuable than gurus'. Models, concepts, and tech-

Self-Directed Learning

- Developmental opportunities come to evolving managers via real-world situations and circumstances. Although general direction (targeted development options) is contracted, the evolving manager's ability to operationalize learning is consistent with his or her abilities, knowledge, education, and experience.

- Targeted development is guided and monitored by coaches, mentors, or sponsors; however, evolving managers' real-world experiences are the teachers and shapers of managerial growth. What *is* is

niques are shared. What ought-to-be is communicated, even simulated to a degree.

- Classroom settings serve as information distribution centers. Transmitting *facts* and *how-to*'s (the latest gospel) is the design focus.

- Preparing to do and practicing how to do constitute what is learned. Live ammo is not used.

- Generally, performance is not tested or evaluated. Sometimes pre- and post-tests are used, mostly for diagnostics or self-scoring. Happy sheets (course evaluation sheets distributed to participants at the close of a workshop and used to assess the quality of a training experience) are common. Assessment centers and other simulations move the training a few steps closer to the real world.

learned. What *can be* is imagined from experienced eyes.

- Applying skills, education, knowledge, and experience is the focus in this problem-centered approach. Designing in daily doses of reality through guided real-world projects is the objective. Reality testing in the trenches is the school yard.

- Trial-by-fire ensures immediate transfer of learning. The evolving manager faces real bullets.

- Feedback on performance occurs daily. The swamp hasn't been drained. The alligators are real. Testing is immediate. Evaluation is swift. Answers come slowly. Challenges come quickly. The workplace is an incomparable classroom, and experience a memorable teacher.

The prescriptions in this targeted development book fall on the self-directed side of learning. Our experience as human potential consultants has shown us that self-direction deepens the learning. Psychological readiness and professional maturity are accelerated. Self-confidence is quickened and sustained. Skills of inquiry become more sophisticated and polished. Survival skills become familiar friends. Decision-making and problem-solving skills become precisionlike and consummate. Creativity is enhanced. Professional worth is built on solid (and hard-fought) developmental ground.

Our bias for self-directed managerial growth will be quite

evident throughout this guide. We make no apology for that. The future of any organization—large or small—depends on leaders who are the products of the mix between self-directed inquiry and formal classroom and training experiences; who have been *groomed* for success on the firing line; who have been shaped by the careful guidance (and extraordinary patience and wisdom) of coaches, mentors, and sponsors along the road to managerial excellence. We hope you'll see enough wisdom in this book to trust us. As for our trusting *you*, we have faith that you will enter this self-directed journey with an open mind, a willing heart, unmitigated enthusiasm, and an insatiable desire to develop extraordinary leadership skills. We believe you can do it. We believe you must. The alligators are real!

The PRESCRIPTIONS

Empowering People

Developing solid team relationships gives any organization a competitive advantage. More and more, today's savvy managers realize that the demands of the marketplace make team relationship development one of the critical survival skills of the 1990s.

When highly motivated, confident, goal-directed, and resourceful team players commit themselves to measurable results, an organization's competitive posture and profitability dramatically increase. A recent American Management Association study of employee job satisfaction indicates that many employees rank work relationships and salary equally. In another related study, by Rosabeth Moss Kanter, author of *The Change Masters,* researchers found that if people understand what is expected and believe they are valued as legitimate team members, they'll drive themselves to unbelievable excellence.

Make no mistake about it, leaders who cultivate a sensitivity toward personal dignity and worth, instill a sense of fair play, and demand depth of commitment at all levels within the organization will enjoy phenomenal success. The prescriptions in this series will help you build a work environment that features a climate of trust, unfailing commitment, and integrity as bone-deep beliefs. It will provide the ongoing developmental mechanism you need to help ordinary people achieve extraordinary results. The fundamental message here is that people have a compelling, natural thirst to be engaged, to grow, to honestly contribute, and that truly involved people can do anything. Truly involved managers will reap unprecedented benefits—with a little help from their friends.

You'll be transformed by these activities. You'll be humbled by some—and deepened. Each prescription will work if you work, so get involved! And if you happen to complete all of these development activities—don't worry! We'll write more!

1. Celebrate small wins

Find at least one tiny event to celebrate each week. It can be someone's birthday or personal accomplishment outside of work—but preferably, some positive accomplishment at work. The minicelebration doesn't have to be a dinner at an expensive restaurant. It can be a box of candy, a package of cookies, applause, or a lusty group cheer. Hold the appreciation banquet at the employee's work station in full view of admiring peers. Thank the group for their support in making this small win possible. Ceremoniously, lead in the cheer and applause. It'll make a world of difference in morale, team spirit, and—believe it or not—productivity. Setting a climate that focuses on positive reinforcement will bring positive results. So often employees hear only what they do wrong. The issue: enhancing morale and building rapport. Keep it up! How long? No more than thirty or forty years. (Caution: Be sure to share the wealth among *all* the employees when celebrating or giving praise. The one who may deserve it the least may be the very one you will reap the greatest benefits from as a result of a Standing Ovation.)

2. Junk-pile management

Write or type at the top of postcard-sized paper the following statement: "The most demeaning, annoying, and humiliating rule/procedure/form/regulation/policy with which I must live is . . ." Call your people together in groups—all the same level in each group (i.e., hourly, new hires, line managers, professionals, etc.). Spend all morning leading the group in a no-nonsense discussion designed to enlist their support in identifying ridiculous rules. Allow the group free and uninterrupted disclosure. Record each demeaning rule, every annoying regulation on chart paper. (This takes guts. If you don't want to know, don't ask!) Then have the courage to change something on the spot! Modify or eliminate a humiliating regulation and you'll endear yourself to the troops. Commit to the changes. Applaud the group's honesty. Then promise rapid action on the rest. Ask for the group's input on fix-its. Unless you visibly demonstrate your commitment within ten working days, you'll lose momentum—and credibility. If one (or more) of your own pet rules is a prime candidate for the junk pile, donate it willingly. Then make long-term and short-term plans—both remedial and proactive. Ask yourself: what was it about the defunct rule/procedure/ form/regulation/policy that annoyed the troops? How was it demeaning? How did it interfere with job performance, job satisfaction, or customer responsiveness?

Repeat this exercise regularly. The odds are you'll begin to build work relationships on trust and commitment to shared objectives. Your days as cop and referee may be over. Congratulations! Is there anything else you'd like to toss onto the junk pile? Our experience is wholly consistent with this point: Once you commit to the process, you'll find immense personal satisfaction and revitalization. This simple token of your willingness and openness to change will lead to vast avenues of improvement and growth.

3. Monitor progress through fireside chats

Organize informal, quarterly forums with your people to discuss "how we're doin' " as a team. Not to be confused with traditional staff meetings, these high-energy sessions should be intensive dialogues between you and your staff. No living, breathing *outsiders* and their interests are permitted to intrude on these fireside sessions. Trust, listening, honesty, empathy, and ethics are the tools that'll make or break these sessions. Asking for gut-level feedback from everyone—receptionist as well as design engineer—legitimizes your obsessive pursuit of excellence. (You are obsessed with excellence, aren't you?) Your greatest advances in competitive positioning will come from initiating these rap sessions routinely, where you ensure constant eyeball-to-eyeball contact with everyone who works with you. Staying in touch with the heartbeats and palpitations of every person in your area of responsibility communicates your commitment— and loyalty—to them. Under the deceptively simple heading of Fireside Chats lies a major concept that brings this guide into crystal-clear relief—achieving incrementalized excellence for sustained professional development through a system of organized daily doses of corporate reality.

What we're suggesting here is to get in touch with your people. Being in touch means just that—letting them see you sweat, hear your unmitigated concern, feel your uncompromised sincerity, taste your unshakable enthusiasm. Do that and you'll experience the Holton Advantage—helping ordinary people achieve extraordinary results!

4. Expect the best

The import of the next question is such that to bury it in a laundry list of questions might minimize its impact. We'd like you to adjourn to a quiet, relaxing place, one that will assure you an uninterrupted thirty to forty-five minutes. The question: If you could get everyone in your organization to outperform himself or herself in one area, what would it be? We feel it's only fair to tell you that some executives can answer that bombshell immediately while others have a little more difficulty framing it. Now fully describe, as completely as time will allow, how you expect to permeate your organization (department, division, unit) with the gospel according to —you! Record your thoughts in writing. What is the essence of your message? Reduce it to one powerful, well thought-out sentence. Now preach your gospel. Consider whether you're walking your talk. If you are, step lively and talk your walk.

5. Crystallize your mission

At your next staff meeting include just one overhead transparency: a copy of the company's mission statement, sales strategy, total quality management announcement, or customer satisfac-

tion promise. Use no other overheads. Just this one. As soon as
the group is ready, switch the projector on and just stand there
quietly. Don't say a word. Wander, slowly and deliberately,
throughout the room. Take your time. (Five minutes will be
quite sufficient—it'll seem interminable.) If handled right, this
could be a galvanizing event. This one simple demonstration,
this snapshot of a vision, is worth not just a thousand words, but
more like a million. Still speechless, let 'em see your sincerity,
your concern, your intensity. Now address your captive audience with an air of humility tinted with an obvious bias for
action. Ask the following two questions in the order in which
they appear, as passionately, as arrestingly as you can: What are
we doing that gets in the way of achieving that goal? (Pause)
What am I doing to sabotage it?

Stand there silently and wait for the first glimmerings of the
group's reaction. You may not have to wait long. On the other
hand, you may have to wait 'em out. Devote as much time as it
takes, even if it takes all day. Simply listen. Let the troops talk.
Record everything that's said. Use a red felt-tip marker to record
the group's input for emphasis. They'll probably draw blood.
(We referred to humility earlier.) Exercise humility now; delegate the task of recording what is said to no one! Record every
word, each assault, every indictment and innuendo, each shot or
salvo leveled by the group, at the group, or directed at you! Say
nothing during the onslaught. Absolutely nothing. Even if the
silence between barrages becomes deafening, remain poised
and quiet, ready to add more fuel to an already brilliant flame.
(Call out for lunch if you have to.) Seem too dramatic? You
betcha. Consider the alternative. Does it make good business
sense to continue operating in full knowledge (or at least sus-
pecting) that your folks are rowing in different directions?

Once you're comfortable with the input, once you've sensed
group catharsis, and after you believe you've heard from everyone—thank the group. Then ask for five to seven volunteers
to join you in addressing each item drawn in blood. Promise to
clean up *your* act first, then tackle the group's shortcomings.
Disregard those items where the group pointed fingers at sabotage artists outside the group. Let the group *own* their mistakes
and shortcomings. Promise quick and decisive remedial action

on two to three items by the close of business that day. Launch a full-blown remedial campaign to eliminate the rest of the mission stoppers. Resolve to make this a team effort. Demonstrate your unmitigated support. Conduct "how are we doing" sessions. Allow team members to lead these sessions. Demand course-correction results. Hold these sessions regularly until the way you do business is in direct alignment with the mission statement. It is extremely important that you show your visible support. Do it unfailingly.

6. Acknowledge shining moments

Organize corporate bragging sessions. Provide an upbeat forum for employees at all levels to share war stories and brag about how successful their units (department/divisions/field operations) were in meeting or exceeding defined objectives. There is a compelling body of team development research that supports this type of activity. Sustained loyalty, commitment, and interest in the job occur when feedback is consistent and timely. The literature on motivation suggests that people tend to repeat behavior they are rewarded for. Make no mistake about it, people will repeat behavior they see as personally and professionally profitable. Reread the last four sentences. One more time. It makes good business sense, doesn't it? Reward superior job performance and you'll get superior job performance. Fail to appreciate or acknowledge heroic actions, and mediocrity results.

   Here's how to organize these snapshots of success. Advertise these bragging sessions (departmentwide, companywide) and hold them quarterly. (If they are held less frequently, continuity and momentum are lost; more frequent sessions, on the other hand, become too time-consuming and routine to keep their novelty status.) Require themes for each session (ways we served our customers heroically, interdepartmental cooperation, new service or product innovations, cost reductions, revenue enhancement, sales and manufacturing partnerships, quality improvements, and so on.)

Offer rewards for the best-judged success story. Have team members vote. Then select a team to compile the best of these shining moments into a company album, history of excellence, small-wins portfolio, or a monthly newsletter designed specifically to praise excellence in productivity improvement, service distinction, quality enhancement, and relationship development. Organize an Annual Shining Moments Banquet. Invite key people from other departments as guests. Include the chief executive and other senior staff. Challenge other divisions to follow suit. Sell reluctant dragons and other holdouts on the idea.

We speak from personal experience when we report that with each small-win-induced transformation, every incremental toast of performance, each shining moment (reported proudly and often), the glimmerings of an evolving mechanism for sustained employee involvement and long-term profitability will begin to emerge.

7. Appreciate people now and avoid the rush

Start a quiet campaign of writing thank-you notes to two or three people each week. Compliment each person on some area of personal or professional development. Your observations could stem from praising people in the areas of risk taking, telephone professionalism, additional education or training received, handling a tough customer, joining a professional society, social or community involvement, working extra hours to ensure meeting a project deadline, resourcefulness, assertiveness, task focus, awards for an achievement, and so forth.

Taking the time and energy to personalize your appreciation will speak volumes. This *hurray-for-you* type of acknowledgment is well worth the minute or so it takes. Don't fail to jot down a few compliments. We contend that this intrinsic motivation is the stuff corporate profitability is made of! We also believe that two types of people respond well to compliments: men—and women! So you can't miss. You'll begin to notice an interpersonal warming and a growing closeness once people feel appreciated. Acknowledge achievements of people in other departments and you'll find an increase in interdepartmental cooperation and understanding. That'll take courage. They'll probably wonder what you're up to. You'll also notice an appreciable increase in your ability to give and receive positive feedback. So go ahead, appreciate them now, and avoid the rush.

8. Training is not a staff infection

Respond to this statement: Training is not a staff infection. Using at least five typewritten pages (lines a space and a half apart), give ten legitimate reasons in support of the above statement. We've provided a few food-for-thought questions to get you started. Why train in the first place? What is the linkage between training and job performance? How do you ensure the transfer of learning from the classroom to the workplace? What types of follow-up take place after the training event? What is the relationship between training and performance appraisal? Is training a line function or a staff infection? How do you measure return on investment? What responsibility does the manager of the employee who attended the training have in ensuring sustained development? Who decides what to train, whom and when? Describe the match between training and identified needs. Who's responsible for training? What's the difference between training and education?

    Tough questions? You betcha! Spend quality time on this activity. Why? We believe that one of the most (if not *the* most) commonly practiced crimes in industry today is a fundamental insensitivity toward ensuring direct transfer of learning from

classroom to the workbench. Tuned-in, turned-on employees
are infectious. Given enough respect and the right kind of training and development, employees will produce unbelievable
excellence.

9. Perform a derailment profile

Perform a postmortem on a project, operation, or new product
idea that failed. It doesn't have to be one in which you were
personally involved. Construct a derailment profile. Examine
the preconditions: development or design cycle, use of resources, planning, work measurement, communication pathologies, turfism, protectionism, task vs. people obsession, guiding
ideology (vision), expectations, depth and quality of management involvement and support, assumptions and other frozen
evaluations, implementation strategy, team makeup, incentive
system, problem-solving and decision-making expertise, time
and money management, organization, member roles and responsibilities, type of organizational support, consistencies and
inconsistencies, managing disagreement, bureaucratic snafus,
chain of command issues, attitude, and other elements.

Compose a What-Did-We-Do-Right/What-Did-We-Do-Wrong
scenario. Meet with the members of the battered project team.
Discuss improvements and fix-its.

10. The pride is back

Observe twenty-five instances of the following good attitudes
and achievements: company pride shown by colleagues during
a one-week period of service above and beyond the call of duty,

respect shown to another employee, exemplary teamwork in action, uncommon courtesy shown to customers, interdepartmental cooperation and camaraderie, heroism, extraordinary attention to ordinary things.

Catalog those instances where people wear their commitment—and passion—on their sleeves, day in and day out. Create a Pride Is Back mechanism (quarterly newsletter, quarterly contest with awards presented, bulletin board publicity, and the like). Determine how to reproduce these prideful moments. Describe the circumstances that produced the exemplary behavior. What was the relationship between task and people?

People tend to repeat behavior they are rewarded for. Hammer that statement into your managerial mind. You want to see twenty-five more instances of pride, don't you? Reward it! Whether we're looking at billion-dollar corporations or three-person operations, we have witnessed demonstrations of genuine pride shown by people who somehow muster up the courage—in spite of doubt, job description, or limited resources—to go the extra mile. Applaud it. Expect it. Acknowledge each act of pride. Celebrate each shining moment.

We agree with Norman Lear, who wrote in the May 20, 1984, issue of the *New York Times*:

> America is suffering from an unhealthy emphasis on success as measured by the Numbers. The tendency to boil the world down into analytic abstractions distorts and oversimplifies the richness of life. It insists upon evaluating the world through ratings and lists, matrices and polls, the bottom-line, winners and losers . . . When . . . business . . . overlooks the human essence, that spirit that defies the marketplace and its economic calculus of motives, it does so at its own peril.

This activity is worth your time and effort. Uncovering these distinctive moments of pride helps determine if yours is an environment where positive things happen often—or rarely. The good news? You can collect these snapshots of excellence now. The bad news? You'll lose them if you don't reward them.

11. Build solid support networks

We have never met a truly successful manager who didn't credit much of that success to the support received from other people. Developing and maintaining a strong network is a critical factor in managerial growth, and must become a constant priority. We'll illustrate this with a beautiful analogy. Have you ever had the opportunity of visiting a magnificent redwood forest? These trees are gigantic! They punch holes in the sky two hundred— even three hundred—feet high! One particularly large tree has a hole cut in its trunk large enough for cars to drive through! Trees of this colossal size, we reasoned, must have really deep root systems. We discovered to our surprise that redwoods get their nourishment from surface moisture. Their root systems are very shallow. How, then, do these trees maintain their stability? They don't stand alone! Their root systems interlock and inter-twine into a vast patchwork quilt of tentacled roots. When winds and storms come, those incredible redwoods stand solid, be-cause they support and sustain one another.

What a developmental lesson we can learn from the red-woods! We need to "spread our roots" and interlock and inter-twine with other people. We challenge you to evaluate your current network. Take steps to strengthen it. Here are the key areas where you need people in your network. Jot down the names of individuals who meet these needs for you. These people are your emotional scaffolding. Your spark plugs. Your personal gurus. Your drill sergeants. Your information liaisons. Your friends.

The six types of people you'll want in your network are

1. *Close friends* who love and support you in spite of your fallacies.
2. *Energizers* who motivate you when the going gets tough.
3. *Experts* who provide information and expertise in your field.
4. *Challengers* who force you to stretch yourself to new heights.

5. *Mentors* who already *are* where you want to go professionally.
6. *Access providers* who help you cut through red tape and gain access to the resources you need.

Two key issues you'll need to address to maximize your network are

1. Does the same person's name appear for each area? This means you're counting on one individual to meet many of your network needs. This is not fair to either you or that person. It places too much of a burden on him or her and can lead to relationship burnout very quickly. Expand your network. Spread out your roots and involve other people.
2. Are there "gaps" where you can't identify anyone who currently fills one of the six roles for you? This indicates a "vulnerability area" for you. Take immediate steps to deputize individuals who can fill the void.

Developing your "Forest of Redwoods" is not a one-shot deal. It is a constantly evolving process. You'll find people moving in and out of your network as your needs (and theirs) change. We urge you to do regular maintenance checks on your network to keep the relationships active, relevant, and healthy. And we'd be remiss if we didn't emphasize the cardinal rule of networking: What you send out will come back—multiplied. Networking is a two-way street, and you must actively help others if you expect help in return. Reciprocate. Accommodate. Escort a colleague through a crisis. Sniff out opportunities to help. It's also helpful to remember the folks in your network with thoughtful notes, cards, and visits when you *don't* need their help. That type of "regular feeding" will keep your forest growing.

We've found that a well-maintenanced redwood support system will literally skyrocket individuals through hard times and catapult them up the ladder of success. You'll meet with uncommon success—with a little help from your friends. So we urge you to plant the seeds today for the trees of tomorrow's forest. Surround yourself with people who believe in you and want to see you succeed. You're known by the company you keep! So

build your network of redwoods! Interlock your talents. Weave
your insights. Enjoy phenomenal success and sustained health
and happiness.

12. Show and tell

This targeted development activity isn't as easy as it appears.
(We can assure you.) Schedule a four-hour meeting one morning. Ask your staff to come prepared for a *roll-up-your-sleeves*
session. Instruct them to bring notepaper. Have a continental
breakfast served. Call out for lunch, too, since four hours is the
minimum time allowed for this staff development activity. Once
you've handled the administrivia and logistics, set the date and
personally conduct the meeting. Make no mention of the agenda
or the reason for the meeting other than to state that for four
hours the group will be involved in an important project.

The purpose of the meeting will be to view a full-length
movie on videocassette. Each member of the group is to take
copious notes. Record impressions and insights. Draw analogies
between the issues raised in the movie and those that occur in
the world of work. Focus on communication issues. Leadership
orientations. Expectations. Giving and receiving feedback. Motivation. Problem solving. Sense of mission. Information flow.
Task vs. people issues. Negotiation skills. Power and influence.
Cooperation. Commitment. Loyalty. Pride. Responsibility. Accountability. Honesty. Ethics.

Any one of the following movies will do very nicely as a
catalyst for group discussion: *Bridge over the River Kwai,
Twelve Angry Men, Rocky, Top Gun, Dead Poets Society, The
Hunt for Red October, Tucker, Rainman, Driving Miss Daisy,
The Sting, Nine to Five, Broadcast News, Children of a Lesser
God, Dances with Wolves.*

13. Clarify who does what

Your sense of competence and value depends on your definition of who you are professionally—whether you're the senior vice president of a billion-dollar industry or the maintenance supervisor of a retirement community. A computer systems analyst or strategist. Robotics engineer or innovation consultant. Experienced or new. Coffee-driven or orange-juice-activated. Manufacturing manager or sales executive. First-line supervisor or main-line CEO.

When people become members of a work group, they are expected to fulfill certain obligations and to perform tasks that are important to the group's effectiveness. When people understand what is expected and believe they are valued as legitimate team members, they'll drive themselves to unbelievable excellence. And that's our point: People have a compelling, natural thirst to be engaged, and truly involved people can do anything. It comes as no surprise then that roles and responsibilities must be clearly defined. Role definitions must be crystal clear. Outlined precisely. Molded and remolded. Negotiated and renegotiated. Agreed upon. Set. Measured. Respected.

When highly motivated, confident, goal-directed, and resourceful team players commit themselves to measurable results, an organization's competitive posture and profitability dramatically increase. The purpose of this *developmental laboratory* is to help your team members recognize their roles, obtain constructive feedback from colleagues on how their role is perceived, and assess how an individual's contributions affect the group's overall performance. This activity is designed for mature work groups and should not be used when team members have limited collaborative experience or are all new hires.

Turn to Vehicle Parts Sheet (Exhibit 1). Introduce the activity as an opportunity for team members to clarify roles and to practice giving and receiving feedback. Distribute copies of the Vehicle Parts Sheet to each employee. Read aloud the definitions of the roles played by the various mechanical and electronic parts of the automobile. Ensure that all team members understand the vehicle descriptions. Distribute copies of the Vehicle Inspection Work Sheet (Exhibit 2). To ensure anonymity, ask all members *not* to write their names on their work sheets. Instruct the team to write the name of any group member (including themselves, if appropriate) next to the number corresponding to the specific car part, or parts, that best define that co-worker's role or contributions to the team. More than one colleague's name may be used for one part. Collect the Vehicle Inspection Work Sheets as soon as everyone has completed the role assignments.

Hold a fifteen- to twenty-minute intermission. Record the information on the Parts Is Parts Summary (Exhibit 3) using chart paper or an overhead transparency. You may want to ask a colleague to serve as scribe while you read aloud the role assignments. When the group has reassembled, begin a discussion on the importance of clarifying roles, responsibilities, and performance expectations, and rewarding exemplary contributions. Ask the group to share their reactions to the group feedback as it relates to group synergy and effectiveness.

Encourage group discussion by asking the following questions: What analogies can we draw from the relationship between a high-performance car and a high-performance work group? If we really were parts of a car, would we sit proudly in a showroom or collect rust or dust in a junkyard? Explain. How has each auto part or accessory enhanced or limited our team performance? In what areas is there a good match between an employee's skills and organizational needs? In what areas do we need maintenance and repair? A tune-up? Touch-up? An overhaul? Diagnostic checkups? Where are we going forward? In reverse? Uphill? Coasting? Hugging the curves? Running off the road? Missing the turnoffs? Outrunning the competition? Lagging behind?

Establish new group norms of excellence. Perform the necessary maintenance and repair. Buff and shine the heroes. Reposition the mirrors and bucket seats. Clean the windshield. Redefine roles with unmitigated clarity. (Including your own role.) We'd like to help you. It's a good place to start, don't you think? We subscribe to the definition Tom Peters preaches. We hope you like it. We trust you'll take it seriously. He said at the beginning of his book:

> For the last twenty-five years, we have carried around with us the model of Manager as cop, referee, devil's advocate, dispassionate analyst, professional, decision-maker, naysayer, pronouncer. The alternative we now propose is leader . . . as cheerleader, enthusiast, nurturer of champions, hero finder, wanderer, dramatist, coach, facilitator, builder.
>
> Peters, Tom, and Austin, Nancy, *A Passion for Excellence*, New York: Random House, 1985, pg. 265.

We'll lead you in a cheer all our own. Right on! What Peters and Austin suggest is not an impossible dream. And it certainly isn't the mad ravings of a couple of management consultants who see people-moving as a respectable calling. We've seen it. We've been privileged to see it harvested. It's electrifying. Intoxicating. It's the key to igniting committed and dedicated people. It'll help ordinary people produce extraordinary results.

14. Learn from old-timers

Spend some quality time with retired managers and staff people. Pick up the phone and call 'em. Buy 'em lunch. Interview ten to fifteen of these *organizational treasures*. Shake their loyal hands. Thank them for years of commitment. And for hanging in there during tough times. And for their tears and their forgiveness for any slights (intentional or otherwise) that may have passed their way. Remember the good times. Heroic times. Reminisce. Recollect. Remember their achievements. Their selfless contributions. Their willingness to go the extra mile. Listen! Genuinely listen.

Then seek their wisdom and advice. Pick their brains. Ask their opinion on a pressing business issue. Update them on the latest acquisitions and technologies. Get their seasoned insights on managing people. The right organizational climate. What works. What doesn't work so well. Sales and marketing savvy. Dilemmas of managing participation. Decentralization. Profitability. Responsibility. Accountability. Creativity. Globalization of economies. Industrial growth. Manufacturing inefficiencies. Discipline. Missed opportunities. Extraordinary successes.

Ask for their thoughts on the capacity of the organization to satisfy customer needs by using whatever resources happen to be available. Include a question on retirement benefits. Inquire about the legitimacy of training and development activities. Personnel. Human Resources. Quality assurance. Talk about organizational communication. Turfism. Staff meetings. Project teams. Employee involvement. Management support. Effective leadership. Service pathologies. Product failures. Quality of work life.

Include their spouses. It's always been a family affair. Ask for their input. Respect their feelings—because feelings are real. People want to feel appreciated. Needed. Valued. The evidence keeps coming in—learn from people who have been there before.

What we're suggesting here is hardly a new idea. It's been around awhile. It's just not done, that's all. The bias seems to be to turn 'em out to pasture. Let the new blood in. In all fairness though, some progressive organizations do invite old-timers back as postretirement consultants. At least for a while. Until they have siphoned off the last bit of knowledge and skill they need to effect a smooth business transition. The timing is usually right, though. The retired executive is generally ready to call it a day, too. His or her managerial worth has been confirmed. Immortality established.

Learn from these old-timers. Listen. Absorb their wisdom. Apply what you can. The curative powers are enormous. The difference it'll make in your managerial worth will astound you. Deepen you. Polish you. You'll stand taller. You'll feel more complete.

15. Treat yourself to an Indiana Jones experience

Organize an adventure weekend. Invite colleagues who glow with challenge. Mobilize around a theme (risk taking, communication, teamwork, decision making, innovation, group synergy, and so forth). Punctuate the experience with shared objectives and legitimate learning outcomes. Hire professional help if the activity warrants it. Infuse the group with team spirit. Garnish it with a sense of mission. Invite the site manager. Seek to include as many managers as you can in your Indiana Jones adventure.

We have found the following adventures to offer plenty of challenge (That's putting it mildly; several have awesome transformative potential): white water rafting, mountain climbing, fire walking, low- and high-element ropes courses, white water canoeing, cross-country cycling, spelunking, base jumping, skydiving (or the more tame, parachuting), cliff scaling, big-game hunting (with camera only), hang gliding, marathon hikes through rough terrain, cross-country skiing, team triathlon, scuba diving for lost treasure.

Treat yourself and a few colleagues to a life-changing event. Experience the thrill of victory and the agony of tired feet. Leave self-doubt behind. Take a sense of adventure. Consult with your family doctor before you go. If you see Indiana in your travels, tell him we said "Hi."

16. Replace talk with action

Substitute quick-hit pilots and prototypes for lengthy proposals. Replace talk with trial runs and tests. Find trial sites and field champions for new service or product ideas. Test an idea now (at least a little chunk of it). Don't wait. Strike some sparks. Ready—

Fire—Aim. The objective of this developmental activity is to pilot-test, then submit a strong proposal based on an already well-defined initial success.

The scenario goes something like this: There is a slow, methodical, low-level (almost invisible) start. A tiny inkling of things to come. This toe-in-the-water beginning is followed by a wildly enthusiastic launch, fueled by word of mouth and roll-up-your-sleeves work from the field. The thing seems to be working. Excitement builds. Most pieces of the maverick program have been field-tested (piloted) already. Momentum builds. Kinks are worked out. Wrinkles smoothed. Refinements orchestrated—proudly and passionately, we might add. Colleagues leap onto the bandwagon, insisting that their operation host the next pilot for this innovative *field*-designed product development (service enhancement, quality assurance, productivity improvement, sales enrichment) program.

Most proposals, as you know, fall victim to endless, hypothetical debate. After all, no support data exist to give it a fair hearing. It just makes good business sense to build a ground swell, using small, strategically placed pilot projects in the field, supported by field champions. This strategy turns out to be one of the most effective—bold, and cost-effective—ways to implement anything.

This *pilot-test-modify-test again-fail-reexamine-test-scrap-begin again* proposal-building method will bring you the hard evidence you need to sell your idea. This approach is scientific. It's field-tested empiricism at its best. It's data-driven and field-activated. Proposal churning pales by comparison. Speculation gives way to hard data. What-ifs become mute in the face of already-dones.

Ready. Fire the furnace of field-to-headquarters involvement. *Aim* for a 50-percent reduction in the time it takes to launch an initial tangible test for an average project, training module, pre-test market, software subsystem, market niche, and so forth. Field-test, then propose. Field-test, then propose. Field-test. Propose. Field-test again.

17. Fail forward

Personally support small failures privately and publicly. The failed efforts we're talking about are those faithfully executed, quickly modified, and thoroughly learned from attempts by ordinary people to achieve extraordinary results. Reward fast failures with a sincere smile, a hearty handshake, and unfailing support. We're not asking you to condone sloppiness, tolerate slipshod work, permit untidiness, overlook intentional carelessness, or the like. On the contrary, we encourage you to applaud honest attempts that go awry. Increase your failure rate. Speed up failure and you accelerate success. Our point is this: Human errors are inevitable—especially when something new and complex is being undertaken. So, for goodness' sake, hurry up and get them over with—now when they're small and manageable.

Each month hold Fail Forward meetings. Start with your own most interesting slipups. Ask colleagues to follow suit. Laugh about it. Emphasize what was learned. Ignite how-did-you-fix-it-so-it-won't-happen-again talk. Hoard each account of a screwup. Ask how we can fail forward faster on Project X or Objective Y. Award prizes for the most hilarious, embarrassing, creative, and useful foul-ups. Convince colleagues to hold similar meetings with their staffs. Hold annual Fail Forward awards banquets.

This prescription can operate very nicely adjacent to the do-it-right-the-first-time quality-assurance plea. Really! Here's how. Doing it right the first time and the quest for constant improvement both acknowledge that each assignment (routine or otherwise) has within it endless opportunities for improved quality. Suppose you're doing something routinely "right" every time and find that you were regularly failing (and didn't know it because you didn't tinker often enough to discover it was broken months—even years—ago). Routineness doesn't mean perfection any more than mistakes mean imperfection.

This prescription boils down to applauding tactics for institutionalizing a bias for action by accelerating the pace of honest failure. The only positively sane approach—to avoid the embarrassment of mammoth program failures is to encourage (institutionalize, nourish, harvest, control) little ones. Small-scale failures that are repaired and used as building blocks soon evaporate. The cumulative effect of small failures, swept out of sight long enough, will trip up even the most worthy of organizations. Not to reward fast failures is a sure recipe for disaster.

18. Seek windows of opportunity

During the next six months, organize a special study team of seven to ten first-line managers (include newly appointed, wherever possible). Visit at least ten businesses (operations centers, profit centers, headquarters sites). These organizations do not have to be similar to yours. Adopt at least ten things they've done *right* that your organization doesn't do well. Implement two immediately, and gain approvals to implement the rest as soon as they fit and timing linkages are set. Consider how ready your organizational culture is to embrace these changes. How palatable are the newly discovered gems? Will their settings hold? At what pace will they shake loose? How valid are these rough-cut measurements? What can be adapted? Fused? Macadamized? Seeded? Ask these questions, and more. Iron out implementation plans.

Consider how well the organizations you visited handle the following: presupervisory training, employee involvement, initiative taking, risk taking, maintenance and minor repairs, housekeeping, safety, capital and operating spending, innovation, measuring and monitoring results, assessing new technology, managing change, recruiting and hiring, responding heroically to customers, transferring learning from the classroom to the work floor, operationalizing incentive pay and benefits packages, assuring quality, developing new employee orientation programs, and so forth.

We believe any manager (first-line, middle-, or top-level) can effect changes in any of the above areas. When supported by a group of quality-conscious colleagues, you can realistically achieve 75 percent of what's advocated here. Start with modest improvements. Settle for nothing less than enhancing the way you do business. Assess each proposed improvement in terms of its contribution to an increased corporate capacity (readiness) for change. Your team's most urgent tasks are to learn from others and welcome change. Demand it. Beg for it, if you have to. As with any of our 101 prescriptions, attitudes are fundamental. This particular prescription is a prerequisite for basic capabilities building, ensuring more operational integrity, and institutionalizing sustained profitability.

19. Hold sunrise services

Organize group discussions around early morning breakfast meetings—at least twice a month. Ask a top manager to keynote each breakfast meeting by being available for questions and discussion. Start with good listeners, and with leaders who really care about people. Invite fifteen to twenty randomly selected employees to attend. Your job is to emcee the meeting. Bill these as no-fault, no-holds-barred, no-information-withheld, *state-of-the-plant get-togethers*. See these as serious opportunities to eliminate any conceivable barrier in what can become a remarkably effective open-door mechanism to build a communication-intensive work environment. You can even use these chats as supplements to more formal (and expensive) attitude surveys.

The key is honest and genuine management visibility and involvement at all levels. Feedback is essential. We know (and so do you) that these breakfast meetings will not ensure instant straight talk. Patience and perseverance will be necessary ingredients in ensuring success. No doubt, the first couple of meetings will be stilted, until employees realize that there won't be any repercussions. Don't schedule an unreceptive manager to meet with the troops—he or she will make a mess of it. Attitude is vital.

Should the company foot the bill for the meals and meeting room? (We recommend you hold these morning breakfasts off-site.) Yes, of course, you should treat the folks to breakfast. Because the *real* menu is filled with entrees such as openness, feedback, listening, relationship building, we-care attitude, you're important, open exchange of ideas, and barrier bashing. What a tremendous return-on-investment for the price of a couple of dozen breakfasts.

20. Organize employee-led visitor tours

Organize a no-nonsense program for employee-directed tours. In practically every organization, there are times when individuals or groups are given permission to tour the physical operations for informational purposes. Typically, these *tourists* are salespeople with customers, public officials, consultants, prospective employees, students, or the general public. Although some guests may be invited to tour for specific technical reasons, most have a general interest in the overall operations. Accurate portrayals of the operations visited are critical to assuring a positive image. No one wants to be associated with a loser. So you'll want to project the kind of image that says we're quality-conscious. Customer-obsessed. Proud. Productive.

Take responsibility for ensuring that every division or department establishes a Good Shepherd of the Month. This must be a voluntary assigment that requires the guides to shepherd the visitors safely and informatively through the division. Design and develop a training package that outlines the responsibilities and qualifications of the guides, anticipate typical questions asked by visitors, tell stories and illustrations about the department, brag of things you're proud of, and outline future plans. (All of this important information must be punctuated with pride. Etched with genuine respect. Deposited with positiveness. Garnished with sincerity. Enriched with honesty. Saturated with integrity. Nourished with loyalty.) Set high standards. After all, these guides represent the company. Visitors will judge you. Form distinct impressions. You'll want these snapshots to be positive. Glowing. Radiantly complimentary. Glazed with success.

Consider granting each guide limited authority to request colleagues to ensure good housekeeping on the day of the visit. Ask colleagues to show the guides unmitigated respect during the tour. Deputize guides who are good corporate citizens, who recognize the importance of impression management, who truly believe that the services you provide and the products you sell are the best available anywhere.

Several spin-offs from this program are worth mentioning. Employee gains are obvious: heightened appreciation for the functional roles and responsibilities of other divisions, a big-picture view of the organization, the bashing of high-walled turfs, ambassadors of good will, builders of rapport, and enhancers of the corporate image.

21. To err is human . . .

Someone once said, "If I learn from my mistakes, then I'm getting a fantastic education!" It's true. Some of the best information can come from a seeming failure, or an embarrassing situation. This strategy is designed to help you put your errors in judgment, your mistakes, your goof-ups, your embarrassments into perspective, and turn them into valuable learning experiences.

Make a list of your most embarrassing situations or your most monumental goof-ups. Now, from the perspective of your experience, review each incident and come up with a moral or lesson to be learned from it. For example, one manager recalled how he had gone into his supervisor's office to discuss a particularly difficult project. He was nervous and leaned against a bookcase for support. The bookcase was not stationary and moved across the room; several books crashed to the floor, and the manager almost fell on his face! The moral of the story: Be sure you draw your support from someone (something) stronger than you are.

We recommend that you keep these insights in a notebook (preferably under lock and key) so that you can review them often. In retrospect, embarrassing situations or failures have valuable lessons to teach us. Often the lesson is peppered with humor that reminds us not to take life (or ourselves) too seriously. How many times have you heard yourself say "Someday I'll look back at this and laugh"? Our immediate, emphatic response: Why wait?

22. Focus on individual differences

One of the biggest challenges facing any team leader is dealing with conflict in a team. Invariably, when a team is formed, cliques will develop. When team members focus on differences, animosity and infighting will result, and this can sabotage a team's effectiveness faster than Monday follows the weekend!

We encourage you to use either of the following activities with your employees, as prescriptions to confront personality conflicts and help team members recognize that only by working together can the team reach synergy.

1. Brainstorm a list of characteristics that describe people in general. Examples include works on computer, wears glasses, enjoys camping, likes to travel, drinks coffee, has a beard, attends meetings, has contact with customers, and so on. Any word or phrase that describes what people do, like, or have is appropriate. Organize team members into groups of five or six. For each description, the team identifies two team members who have certain similarities, and one team member who is different. If the criterion is "works on computer," then list two team members who work on a computer as part of their job, and one team member who doesn't. For the criterion "drinks coffee," identify two team members who drink coffee, and find one who doesn't. After approximately ten minutes of matching three names with each criterion, analyze the results. Help the group identify any patterns (for instance, was one person always in the "different" column? Did two people always get paired together?). Then focus on the fact that everyone is alike in some ways, and everyone is different in some ways. Emphasize the need to focus on strengths and ignore differences that are irrelevant to team performance.

2. **Group team members into triads (threesomes).** Each triad is then told that they must eliminate one person from their group. They must identify a specific criterion to base their decision on (nonsmoker, different color eyes from everyone else, wearing a different color, and so on). After each group has eliminated a team member, the eliminated members form their own group. Lead a discussion on how selections were made, how each team member felt during the process, how disagreements were handled. Allow the group of eliminated team members to share their feelings about being excluded and put into a group by themselves. If you wish, you can then regroup in different triads and repeat—as many times as you find useful. It's interesting to keep a record of reasons the groups choose to eliminate a team member and who was eliminated from each team. Patterns will emerge that make good discussion starters.

23. Perform a checkup from the neck up

Have you noticed how much emphasis is being placed on team development these days—self-directed work groups, quality circles, participative teams? No matter what labels are used, the message is loud and clear: Today's manager must be able to facilitate team involvement. One of the secrets of team effectiveness is the ability of team members to critique their progress—to make judgments on how well they're doing.

Consider the role critique has played in your past work experience. Unfortunately the scenario usually looks like this: A project gets derailed. Something goes wrong. Derailment profiles are begun. Performances reviewed. Previous decisions analyzed. Evaluations made. People and actions criticized. All attention is directed to what went wrong. The focus is almost always on the product rather than the process. Positive, productive performances (those incremental small wins) are usually buried under tons of accusations, barrages of finger pointing, and paralysis of analysis.

But projects that go well are taken for granted. Exemplary performance ignored. Extra, unsolicited effort unappreciated (or even worse—ridiculed). Positive communication extinguished. Cooperation and loyalty unrewarded.

A Checkup From the Neck Up is a strategy your team can use to grow with, and your own facilitative leadership skill can prosper, too. Following every completed project, meeting, or performance evaluation period, have each team member evaluate team involvement. (Use the questions in Exhibit 4.) Once everyone has had an opportunity to offer his or her critique, pool the results and discuss team perceptions openly and honestly.

Initially you may want to allow team members to share their critique anonymously. Once appropriate levels of trust and honesty are developed, you will want to encourage open sharing of thoughts. This kind of feedback can galvanize a group. It can build phenomenal rapport. Punctuate positive interpersonal relationship development. It can inspire the group. Detonate unbridled loyalty and commitment.

As your team develops, you may want to redesign how you do business. We strongly encourage you also to ask for specific feedback on your leadership ability—what you're doing that the group likes, how you can improve, and so on. Asking for no-holds-barred feedback can be frightening. (We're sensitive to that. Unfailingly so.) This routine checkup from the neck up is serious business—and necessary to ensure sustained productivity, loyalty, and organizational health.

===

24. Uncover value gaps

Whenever two or more people come together, the potential for conflict exists. Most managers shy away from conflict, seeing it as a negative influence on team development. However, we want you to recognize that conflict, in and of itself, is not always debilitating. Conflict can be a stimulating force, stretching the group to explore different concepts and ideas and to challenge old ways of thinking. Only through occasional conflict can a group move from mediocrity and passivity into growth and team mastery. But there is a catch! You have to keep the group focused on the issues, rather than allow conflicts that surface to derail team performance and turn an otherwise smooth operation into a free-for-all personality clash.

Conflicts related to goals, procedures, and interpretation of information are all fairly easy to referee. The tough peace-making job comes when there is a sharp contrast in underlying values. And what's most interesting is that value judgments are often so deeply ingrained into the very fiber of one's personality that the *real* issues perpetuating the conflict are muzzled.

For example, one employee may believe that habitually staying late shows company loyalty and commitment. Another employee who believes he or she is just as committed never stays late because time with family is a strong value.

This prescription will help you and your colleagues appreciate the healthy aspects of conflict and identify the core values shared by team members. Everyone brings his or her own value system (complete with emotional baggage) into the work setting. Every work environment cultivates values of its own, too. When individual and organizational values clash, conflict occurs— often with intense emotions, self-righteous judgments, and unbridled rage. In most cases, underlying value differences remain subtly hidden under emotional masquerades. Hard feelings result. Relationships may sever. Alliances split. Productivity and job performance sputter. Trust and cooperation erode. Exemplary performances go unnoticed.

Two-by-Two is an activity that forces you to make some hard decisions about what is most important to you, and also identify the values rewarded in the work environment. We recommend that you complete the "Two-by-Two" Profile (Exhibit 5) yourself, and then use it with your team members. Through a more complete awareness of value differences and beliefs, team members can discover who they are and how they can cooperate to achieve performance objectives.

The "Two-by-Two" Profile (Exhibit 5) provides a list of paired words or phrases. Develop a working definition for each word or phrase. Then decide which of the two is more descriptive of your belief—which you feel is more important in terms of success and productivity. Using the same working definitions, decide which of the pairings better describes your work environment—what is most rewarded?

Once each team member has completed his or her "Two-by-Two" profile, compile the results. This consolidated profile will reveal what the team values overall and will identify perceptual differences among team members about the work culture. Use the following questions to generate group discussion:

1. Describe what you saw happening as team members reacted to these issues. What things occurred that made it uncomfortable? What behaviors occurred that made things go well?
2. How did you see differences of opinions handled? How was consensus reached in determining what the team values would be? To what extent did majority rules dominate through the decision-making process?
3. Describe the level of participation among team members. Was there overparticipation by some? Underparticipation? How committed were members to this activity?
4. What new insights do you have about team members? About the team as a whole? About me as your manager?

5. How can we deal with differences in personal value profiles versus our newly established team values profile?
6. How does this profile relate to the way we work together? What changes do we need to consider as we integrate personal values with those values we have agreed to as a team.

Modeling Leadership Excellence

Given a little direction, a few resources, and a touch of the dramatic, people will achieve unbelievable excellence. Modeling leadership excellence is fundamental—absolutely essential—for long-term organizational success. Genuine, unadulterated leadership excellence exhibits qualities that are paradoxically interwoven into a diaphanous web, which holds the human spirit secure—and awestruck—at the same time. It is the spark of integration, cementing performance, yet loosening human potential; pulling, yet binding opposites together.

Leadership builds trust—that special dimension that assures those who follow that the one who leads will always act morally, guaranteeing the wellness of each individual. A sense of rightness surrounds the mysterious and charismatic qualities of leadership. A leader's essence is punctuated with uncompromised integrity. Unmitigated fairness. Absolute loyalty. It is infused with sensitivity and compassion. Determination and self-confidence ooze from every pore. It is spurred by a clear sense of mission. Outfitted with insight and decisiveness. Italicized with a love for people and an unwavering sense of duty. Perhaps in its highest essence, leadership recognizes economic, political, and technological realities, yet heeds the stillness of the voice from within, rather than the constant (and sometimes deafening) chatter from without.

We are convinced that there is more leadership in you and in us than we demonstrate. Than we realize. Than we can even conceive! The prescriptions that follow are designed to help you model leadership excellence at every turn. Your experiences will have a galvanizing effect. We hope you'll exemplify leadership excellence. Take responsibility for it—become the total leadership package.

25. Meet the "Pro"

If you want to be a pro at a skill, study what other pros have done; learn from them; do what they do; and you, too, can be a pro! This is the premise that Meet the "Pro" is based on. Identify a specific skill you want to improve, such as generating group discussions in your meetings, managing multiple priorities, starring in undoable projects. Then find someone who is a real pro at that craft. This "Pro" may be someone within your organization or industry; however, don't hesitate to extend your search beyond your own backyard. The world is full of folks who do things well and are more than willing to share their knowledge with others.

Once you have identified your target skill and your Pro, schedule a time when you can observe the Pro in action. Your role is to sit unobtrusively in the background and observe specifically how the Pro handles your targeted skill. Don't get sidetracked by strategies he or she employs in other areas; focus only on how he or she creates the magic in your area of interest. Take copious notes! Do not—we repeat—do not evaluate whether the strategies will work for you. Simply record any and all techniques that work for the Pro.

Following your observation session, schedule a debriefing session with your Pro. The purposes of the session are to share your observations and to get tips and answers to questions such as

- What problems have arisen when you've used these strategies?
- What is going on inside your head as you implement certain techniques?
- How can I make these techniques work for me?
- What initial suggestions do you have for me?
- What are the worst experiences you've had in the context of this targeted skill? What have you learned from your experience?
- What can *I* learn from *your* experiences?
- What other resources would you recommend?

This list only scratches the surface! Your questions will vary, depending on the particular skill you target. We recommend you use a tape recorder (if possible) for this debriefing session with your Pro. Don't waste valuable time taking notes. This is a mountaintop experience, so you want your undivided attention directed at your guru. Review your notes and audiocassette later. Select one or two specific actions you want to implement. Then practice, practice, practice!

26. Use executive dialogues as barometers

Establish a network with other managers who model the leadership qualities you seek to develop. Commit to telecommunications links weekly or monthly, or set quarterly meetings to discuss how to improve interpersonal relationships, manage change, mold and shape subordinates, engineer product campaigns, and so forth. Share examples of your experiences and seek advice and direction from managers who are already savvy in specified areas. You'll know who these experts are. Their actions are consistent. They are the cheerleaders, coaches, and storytellers. They're the ones who communicate unshakable core values by modeling leadership excellence at every turn. In a word, they believe in no-nonsense, face-to-face, eyeball-to-eyeball leadership. Members of your network do not have to be limited to your company. Peer relationships outside your company can be extremely helpful. Moreover, seek candidates who are master *momentum-makers,* who have the uncanny ability to move people toward unbelievable excellence, who consistently and with immense pride empower people to outperform themselves. Use these people as barometers. And their advice as professional "mana." Develop lasting relationships. It's up to you. No contact, no relationship. Draw from the experiences of those whom you respect—those who have been down the lonely, rocky, people-moving road just a few more times than you have.

27. Build your personal library

Purchase the following books: *In Search of Excellence* (Peters and Waterman), *A Passion for Excellence* (Peters and Austin), *Thriving on Chaos* (Peters), *The Service Edge* (Zemke and Schael), *The Renewal Factor* (Waterman), *The Change Masters* (Kanter), *Reinventing the Corporation* (Naisbitt and Aburdene), *Self-Directed Work Teams* (Orsburn, Moran, Musselwhite, Zenger), *Service Within* (Albrecht), *Service America* (Albrecht and Zemke).

That's right, take out your overused checkbook and free up some bucks. Why should you? A couple of reasons: First, you need to genuinely (and visibly) enhance your image of one who is serious about staying current (and interested) in leadership development. After all, you do have a passion for excellence, don't you? Second, your return on investment, in terms of professional growth and revitalization, will be exceptional—if you put your ego aside and realize that there's something you can learn from the reading. (That's right—reading! We do want you to *read* these books. We thought we'd better say this—we don't want to overlook the obvious!)

Each of these texts will stretch you, deepen you, even fascinate you at times. Whatever the level of your executive development, if you don't have these books lining your bookshelves, you're missing out on some of the best management reading in years. Do it now! Buy all ten of them. *Buy* them—don't rent them (you'll want to mark these books up and read them again and again). Totally absorb their messages over the next three to four months.

Make notes in the margins of each book as the spirit moves you. Highlight. Underline. Question. Apply what is learned to your organization's way of doing business. Compare. Assess. Connect. Galvanize. Germinate. Cross-pollinate. Borrow. Cultivate. Capture. Reproduce. Complement. Customize. Endorse. Glamorize. Normalize. Hybridize. Systematize. Replicate. Dream.

28. Organize a Book-of-the-Month Club

Every month, select a book related to your skill development as a manager. We have included a list of Recommended Readings in the back of this book to get you started. But all you need to do is scan the shelves of the Business Section at your local bookstore or library. After you've selected your "Book of the Month," read it! Search for one or two nuggets that you can apply to meeting one of the endless challenges in your department.

Write a critique of each book, summarizing the key points you want to implement or adapt to your work area. Then schedule a meeting with your manager to review your recommendations and discuss implications.

What? We didn't hear you say you don't have time to read a book a month, did we? Aren't you worth the investment of the time it takes to read a few chapters a day? You deserve to be up-to-date on the latest strategies to make your job easier! So sign up now for the Book-of-the-Month Club.

By the way, once you make this a habit, you'll probably become so good at writing summary critiques that you'll want to submit them to your company newsletter, trade journal, or national magazine.

29. Found a peer-level literary society

This is an extension of Prescription 28, Book-of-the-Month Club. We believe that two heads are better than one, and three are better than two! Invite a group of managers who are all interested in their continuing professional development to join you in selecting a book of the month (or quarter, if you just aren't prepared to tackle one a month!). Agree to read the book (in its entirety) and jot down comments, questions, concerns, and recommendations for applying what you've learned. At an agreed-upon time, have the Literary Society meet to discuss the book and share insights.

We've seen this technique literally transform an organization. People get excited when they talk about good ideas. This excitement translates into action, which becomes contagious throughout a department, a division, and the entire organization.

30. Raise your hand if you're sure

Some of the best development experiences come from involvement in special projects in your company or community. We highly recommend that you actively seek opportunities to chair committees or entire projects. By volunteering, you automatically set yourself apart from the pack because most people play hide-and-seek when these projects need help. Once involved, you'll gain unbelievable skills in communication, goal setting, project planning, motivation, time and stress management, networking, financial development, and so on.

The questions that most often pop up when we discuss this strategy are *how* and *where*. First let's talk about how: If you have limited (or no) experience in a particular area, how can you do a credible job while you learn?

- Volunteer first as a committee member—apprentice yourself to the committee chair. Let the chair know that you want to become more involved.
- Talk with others who have been successful on these kinds of projects.
- Review the files from other, similar projects. Learn what worked, what problems were experienced, and how participants were motivated.
- Be creative. Be innovative. Implement new ideas and

stretch your imagination as you work on these projects. Keep a record of what you do, what you've learned, and how you can apply those learnings to your current job.

Next, let's give you a few ideas of *where*. This list is just a start. Opportunities abound for you to raise your hand and get involved:

- United Way campaign
- Company recreation committee
- Community fund-raising projects
- Selected "causes" in which you believe
- Professional organizations (programs, special projects, etc.)
- Church committees
- Employee involvement projects

31. Goal getting is goal setting

You've heard it said that hindsight is always twenty-twenty? This strategy will help you make decisions to bring your foresight into clearer focus. So many times we make thoughtless decisions about our lives and our careers. We let other people define our success, or we simply allow circumstances to make our decisions. For example, we've known managers who, without question, accepted certain career promotions, and then regretted their decisions because the jobs weren't right for them.

As you consider various options in your developmental process, use this technique to help clarify the career choices you make. We recommend you compile your notes in a "Twenty-Twenty Foresight" notebook. It'll measure your progress as you review choices from your past.

1. *Clarify exactly what goal you want to pursue.* It may be a career goal, a certain income level, a material possession, a health or weight goal, a personal achievement goal, or

something else. As you write it, frame it in a positive context. For example, instead of saying "Overcome fear of public speaking," write "Be able to speak in public with confidence and skill."

2. *Now determine how you'll know when you've achieved it.* Be specific. How will it look, feel, and sound when you've achieved the goal? Very often we find that managers are frustrated because they haven't identified what success will look like, so they don't know when they've succeeded. Ask yourself, "What is it about this goal that appeals to me? Why do I want to achieve it?"

3. *What effect will achieving this goal have on your relationships?* Fully consider the implications of this question. It is tougher than it sounds. If you achieve your goal, how will it affect your family? Your friends? Your involvement in civic, church, and extracurricular activities? Your relationships with colleagues? Consider every relationship you have and analyze each goal's impact on that relationship.

4. *Another tough area to consider: What effect will achieving this goal have on you?* What adjustments will you have to make? For example, will the goal, once attained, require you to travel more? Suppose you have to seek more formal education? Relocate? Assume more responsibility for more people? Fewer people? Culturally diverse people? Will losing weight require a new wardrobe? (Sounds great, but unless you are independently wealthy, you'd better plan how to outfit the new you.)

   By considering these issues, you will be able to make intelligent choices. And by knowing why you're making them, you won't resent the impact these changes have on your life-style.

5. *One final question to analyze: What is preventing you from achieving this goal?* Take a good, hard look at yourself and identify any obstacles to your success. This could include lack of education or skills, insufficient experience or finances, personal fears or doubts. As you identify the obstacles, you can begin to plan specific strategies to lessen their impact or even eliminate them.

A friend of ours commented that often what managers *think* they want and what they *really* want are vastly different. This process helps you focus on what you really want, so that you get a big return on your investments of time, resources, and energy.

32. Fortify your influence portfolio

The developmental payoffs resulting from this activity will have a galvanizing effect on your career. Studies of the amount of influence exercised by managers at each level in the authority hierarchy reveal that the most effective (and therefore successful) managers are able to demonstrate skill in several different kinds of influence. This means that their lines of influence are tentacled in many different directions and that they are able to use the right kind of influence at the right time and under the right circumstances.

The purpose of this activity is to help you understand the power of influence and its tangible and intangible benefits in gaining the support you need to more effectively carry out your managerial responsibilities. In a very real sense influence is derived authority. Giving it up becomes difficult at best, and impossible if it must be shared with others with whom you are not compatible in outlook, philosophy, or managerial style. We think you'll agree that each move up the corporate ladder means further concentration of influence and closer proximity to the inner circle of power. The closer you come to the power source, the more accurately you'll be able to see, seize, and wield your own influence.

There are many sources of influence within organizations. We refer to them as *currencies of influence.* (Examples of using your currency include stating exactly what you want or need, clarifying any problems your request may cause, and finding ways to resolve identified concerns or satisfy additional needs another manager may have in order to gain the cooperation and support you need.) In this sense, influence is the currency of action. The more currency, the more action.

How much currency do you have? What sources of influence do you have in your managerial repertoire? We'd like you to examine the source of your influence and then determine the direction you want to go in terms of developing and expanding your currencies of influence. Complete the Influence Profile (Exhibit 6) and the Influence Profile Scoring Sheet (Exhibit 7). Then turn to Currencies of Influence (Exhibit 8) and study the currencies of influence, paying particular attention to your own dominant and backup styles of influence. Examine your Influence Profile. Then answer the following developmental questions: What is your primary influence orientation? Your least used? Your backup style? Were you surprised to find one orientation favored to the detriment of another? How do your most-used influence orientations enhance your ability to manage in terms of information sharing? Cooperation? Interpersonal communication? Project and task movements? Leadership proclivities? How does your distribution of influence hinder or derail your level of achievement? In what specific ways does your primary influence orientation match your functional role in the organization? Determine the influence orientations of colleagues based on your current perceptions of how they *spend* their influence. Analyze them. Fuse them. Etch them clearly in your growing awareness. Meditate on them. Unzip your biases. Choreograph your future moves. Unbutton your aspirations. Fertilize your currencies of influence. Retool, if you have to. Sniff out the benefits. Fortify your influence portfolio with the highest payoff currency.

33. Tighten your funding strategy

Read the last three years of annual reports, quarterly updates, and any other financial reports that your organization publishes. These documents do not generally give budget information.

Nevertheless, the text accompanying the balance sheet and income statement will give you some idea who is getting the credit (or blame) for the organization's profitability. (If your area is never featured, what does that tell you about your power and influence—and corporate status?) Those publications will also highlight forthcoming investments and markets. They also address significant problems and anticipated challenges.

A look at the balance sheet may also give you a better feel for the level of risk and degree of change that senior management will support. If the reports are glossy, study the pictures. For example, if you're in the widget department but all the colored pictures showcase doohickey manufacturing or sales people and projects, you may want to ask yourself some sobering questions. The extent to which an organization chooses to represent itself reveals volumes about its values and what it considers important.

As you look at expanding your internal marketability, you may want to examine how and where your organization spends its money. If your area isn't one of the graced areas, you may consider the somewhat risky strategy of legitimizing your area by showing how profitable it can be and then asking for funding. Do your homework! Couch your funding requests in terms senior managers appreciate. Use *hot button* terminology. For example, if your division chief always reports costs in terms of number of defects eliminated, do the same. If "revenue" or "profit" or "return on assets" are the magic words at the top, explore ways to report your results using similar terms. Decorate your report with silver-tongued language. Mimic. Hybridize. Replicate. Reiterate. Stencil in favorite phrases and words. Align your request with important corporate goals and objectives. After all, aren't your programs important? Don't you want to increase your contributions and value to the organization?

Offer to assist in the financial process. Look at where the marketing and advertising dollars are spent. Ask yourself: What has been approved in the budget over the last couple of years? Disapproved? Which pieces remain uncut? Who got additional funding? When things get tough, who seems insulated from budget cuts? What latitude do colleagues have in actual expenditures? Meet with successful funding wizards. Ask questions. Seek advice. Look for germinal ideas and creative insights. Tattoo all this advice on your funding strategy.

34. Treat people fairly, not barely

How fair and honest are you in evaluating your employees? Most managers like to believe they are unbiased and able to assess people's strengths and weaknesses realistically. They really think they're consistent in managing employees. We challenge you to evaluate yourself. On a sheet of paper, draw a vertical line down the center of the page. Now think of one of your difficult employees—one to whom you find it hard to give negative feedback, with whom you feel a little uncomfortable.

On the lefthand side of the paper, describe what it is about that employee that makes it difficult for you to deal with him or her. What are the characteristics, behaviors, or attitudes that make you uncomfortable?

Next, think of an employee with whom you are very comfortable. Even giving negative feedback is easy for you with this individual. On the right side of the paper, describe the characteristics, behaviors, and attitudes of the employee that make you comfortable.

Now comes the moment of truth. Are you ready? Look at both descriptions and ask yourself, "How am I like the description on the left side?" List any similarities on the lefthand side. Then ask the same question about the righthand descriptions and record your responses.

Notice anything interesting? If you're like most managers, you'll find you are much more similar to the righthand side descriptions than the left. Why? We tend to be more comfortable around people who are similar to us in beliefs, values, attitudes, and behaviors. Conversely, we tend to judge more harshly those who are different from us.

Use this information to analyze your treatment of employees, in terms of consistency and fairness. Take action to overcome any hidden biases you may be experiencing.

35. Deputize a White-Glove Brigade

We shouldn't have to prescribe this. There should be no more obvious management responsibility. If your organization's lobby, offices, customer-contact areas, loading docks, cafeteria, shop, and other work areas look shabby and unkempt—if the toilets are foul and contaminated with graffiti on the walls and stall doors—how can you dare to preach quality? Attention to service? Human dignity? Commitment to the bottom line? Loyalty to organizational goals? Integrity? Respect? Safety?

How can you institute a company pride program by meeting in a dingy, cramped, poorly lighted room the size of a jukebox? How can you allow dust and grime to collect on machinery and equipment and require employees to work safely? When is the last time the employee locker room or shop areas were painted? How modern is your cafeteria? Do the salt and pepper shakers in the canteen work? Are tops of file cabinets piled high with materials? Are vending machines chronically out of order? When is the last time you refurbished chairs and furniture in leisure-time areas?

Demand cleanliness. Deputize a White-Glove Brigade composed of four to five employees from different functional areas and responsibilities. Commission them to become housekeeping fanatics. Design a housekeeping checklist. Obtain the necessary approvals and clout. Poke around in the nooks and crannies of your organization. Report on deficiencies. Involve maintenance and safety. Refuse to allow people to renege on housekeeping requirements and improvements. Establish some mechanism to ensure long-term housekeeping assurance. Don't rule out the dramatic. Nothing else has worked. Right?

Revisit the same areas within forty-five days. Obtain permission to confiscate out-of-bounds materials on countertops and tops of file cabinets. Create a temporary redemption office. *Violators* may redeem items and materials—after they promise to clean up their act.

Does this prescription sound silly? Well, we've got news for you. Poor housekeeping is a block to superior performance. It's an affront to productivity improvement. It's an embarrassment. It compromises quality—absolutely. And sends mixed messages to customers and employees alike. It's just plain unprofessional.

36. Project a professional image

Have a studio-quality business photo made. Ask the professional studio to take several poses. Head shot. Wide shot of talent (that's you) behind—better yet, sitting on—a desk. Full-body shot. Be sure to include any materials or equipment that symbolize what you do. Black-and-white photos are best. Have fifty four-by-five prints made. Incorporate them on thank-you notes, memos, and other correspondence. Use them as promo shots for trade association and convention bulletins and programs that feature you as one of the concurrent session speakers. Include a copy of your photo along with your bio information in the packet you send to a local club president who has engaged you to speak at the next monthly meeting. Send a photo to local or regional newspapers announcing your engagement to speak. Publicize an announcement of a promotion, or career achievement by including a studio-quality photo.

Purchase several eight-by-ten photos. Hang one in your office. Send the message to colleagues that you're proud—and serious—about your professional image. Cast a professional shadow. Dramatize your belief in modeling excellence. Personify success. Imitate the you in the photograph. See it as an endorsement of your professionalism.

37. Let 'em see you sweat

Without hesitating one more minute, build exercise into your daily routine. Go ahead— do a couple of jumping jacks (eight to ten quick ones would be nice) and touch your toes five times. Do it! Before you read any further—We'll wait. Now you can say it—you've exercised today! You've just taken a giant step—if you really did patronize our wishes. We're not being condescending. Committing yourself to exercise is one of the most important decisions you'll ever make. It takes a quantum leap in consciousness.

Launch an exercise program *today* that involves both aerobic and anaerobic conditioning. Before embarking on any fitness program, however, acquaint your physician with your proposed exercise regimen and nutritional plans. The benefits of moderate exercise are well known. There's a ton of research that preaches the life-enriching effects of proper nutritional habits and the right kind of exercise, so we won't preach—except to encourage you to adopt a lifelong health and wellness program now. Begin gently. Build slowly. Be cautious of gimmickry. Look forward to a trimmer, firmer, more healthy you. Manage your health as well as you supervise your work or maintain your automobile.

We won't repeat all the reasons why you should exercise. We won't remind you that compelling research shows that exercise contributes to lessened sick leave, lower turnover, fewer errors, and productivity improvements. You already know that. What you haven't asked yourself is "What is it about *me* that very effectively relinquishes all responsibility for ensuring my own health and wellness and assigns it to someone or something else?" How much longer is it okay for me to abuse my body? Diminish it? Pollute it? Pulverize it? Deprive it of health? Deplete it? Humiliate it? Drain it? Rust it? Refuse to listen when it screams at me to take better care of it?

So opt for the fitness advantage. Let 'em see you sweat.

38. Fifty-two character builders

Leadership excellence is developmental. It is accessible to every manager who wants it. Who really cares enough to go the extra mile. Some of the brightest and best-trained managers we know miss the boat entirely on this score. Leadership takes practice. It evolves. It materializes out of trials and tribulations that build character. It is not—and never will be—legitimized through ledgers, spread sheets, or accountability reports. It comes from the sweat glands of managers who pour their hearts our every day to deliver distinctive service and produce quality products by motivating ordinary people to do extraordinary things.

Good leaders are visionaries. Momentum builders. Productivity engineers. Cheerleaders. Infectious optimists. Dream brokers. They demonstrate unfailing commitment. Uncompromised integrity. Unshakable core values. Unconditional love. Surgical decisiveness. Uncommon maturity. And an unmitigated belief in people's worth.

These are the rites of passage for the exceptional leader. They are the stamps of approval for the evolving manager. To better mold and shape those who follow, the consummate leader must have walked the developmental path a few steps—no, a few miles—ahead.

This prescription asks you, the evolving manager, soberly and with considerable humility, to dedicate the next fifty-two weeks to a close examination of your own character. Your core values. The very essence of your philosophical and thinking nature. Examine the real you.

Develop for each of the fifty-two concepts outlined in this prescription a concise personal definition. Examine one and only one concept each week. Study it. Live with it. Read quotations on the subject by famous people. Look for evidence in your own life—in the lives of others. As thoroughly as possible, sift through the literature. Then pry into your own beliefs and values. Sculpt a definition that you can live with. That you'll *own* as yours.

Collect them in a notebook. One page for each definition. Feel free to modify any definition throughout the year. Jot down insights. Add comments. Play fifty-two pickup at the end of the year—review (in one sitting) every single definition. Then revisit each definition, one at a time, and ask this one gut-wrenching question: "How does my belief about this affect the way I manage people?" Do some soul searching here. Creep into your attitudes. Fish for your deep thoughts, your innermost convictions. Floss to catch hidden assumptions. Probe. Chisel.

Record your thoughts about each definition. Compose a few sentences. Phrases. Words. Formulate action plans designed to help move you toward an exceptional leadership philosophy based on these values. You'll need to work through all fifty-two in order to play with a full deck.

Your deck of fifty-two concepts is outlined below. Work through them in any order. Your matriculation through these foundational concepts will be rewarding and enriching. Cosmopolitan in nature. Philosophically enlightening. Intellectually stimulating. Emotionally deepening. Professionally galvanizing.

Success	Opportunity	Expertise
Failure	Adversity	Leisure
Risk	Choice	Luck
Freedom	Honor	Money
Perfection	Censorship	Time
Trust	Change	Truth
Spirituality	Courage	Wealth
Commitment	Destiny	Wisdom
Fear	Dignity	Wellness
Dying	Power	Vision
Loyalty	Talent	Forgiveness
Pride	Enthusiasm	Conflict
Creativity	Excellence	Competition
Pain	Guilt	Sacrifice
Fame	Habit	Education
Professionalism	Humility	Family
Responsibility	Humor	Justice
Quality		

39. Put your "best look" forward

How important is image to your professional development? Researchers report that people make decisions about your credibility, knowledge, and expertise within the first four minutes of contact. We know it's not fair to judge a person so quickly, but the point is that people do it! Whether it's fair or not is irrelevant. Therefore, we urge you to spend some quality time evaluating and enhancing the professional image you project.

There are three key areas to analyze:

1. Your wardrobe
2. Your work area
3. Your attitude

These three pieces, when joined properly, create a portrait-quality snapshot of professionalism. Let's examine each briefly:

1. Your wardrobe: First, rummage through your wardrobe and discard everything that no longer fits—or doesn't make you feel good when you wear it. We know it's tough to get rid of clothes. But if what you bought isn't the real you anymore, it's only taking up valuable space—and letting clothes hang there only makes you feel guilty for not wearing them. (If you can't fit into them, give 'em away.) Your best image consultant is a full-length mirror and your own honest intuition.

Now, begin to build the professional look you desire. Take a look at the top executives in your company. Watch managers whose image you admire. Observe television celebrities. Peek at magazine advertisements for tips and ideas. Remember, you are *on stage,* so dress for success. And don't forget your feet! Shoes should be shined, cleaned, unscuffed, and well-heeled—so that you look good coming *and* going.

We recommend you have a few pictures taken of yourself before and after you make changes in your appearance. Watch yourself "professionalize" before your own eyes!

RECOMMENDED READING: *Dress for Success*, by John Molloy.

2. Your work area: Walk into your work area right now and snap some pictures! No fair cleaning up or rearranging. We want the real thing. Now, analyze the impression a first-time visitor would get upon entering. Is there a feeling of organization, control, expertise? Or is there an image of clutter, confusion, and disaster? Like it or not, your work area reflects your professionalism. So, clean it up! Canvas the books crowding your bookshelves. What do the book titles say about you and your interests? Examine any quotes or posters and be sure they convey positive messages. (We'll never forget the sign we saw over a Human Resource Manager's desk. It read: "How to Motivate Employees" and had a picture of an employee leaning over the desk with a manager holding a sword over his head. Imagine the image conjured up in the minds of employees—and customers—entering that office!)

Again we recommend before and after pictures. You'll be amazed to find how much more professional you appear with a tidy work area.

RECOMMENDED READING: *The Time Trap* by Alec MacKenzie.

3. Your attitude: Keep a mirror on your desk and observe your facial expression periodically. Managers often make their jobs tougher simply because they look unapproachable and wear a negative attitude every day. Try this exercise: Focus all your attention on both corners of your mouth. Now, at the same time, lift both corners! That's called a smile. Do it often. It's been said that it's our attitude, not our aptitude, that determines our attitude. Build an attitude that is positive, persuasive, and professional.

RECOMMENDED READING: *How to Enjoy Your Life and Your Job*, by Dale Carnegie.

SECTION THREE

Welcoming Change

The corporate capacity for and acceptance of continuous change must be dramatically increased. Every organization needs within itself the means for adapting to a relentlessly shifting environment. Managers must learn to welcome change as vigorously as they fought it in the past. It is simply a powerful, inescapable fact that managers must come to terms with if constructive change and corporate survival are to occur. The means for this change rest ultimately with leaders who must be able to confidently manage chameleonlike corporate landscapes.

Managers operate in a world of rapidly accelerating change which is occurring on many fronts—scientific, political, technological, communications, institutional, and cultural. The work force, too, is changing. We are entering one of those rare periods in history when the economic imperative for a more competitive and productive work force demands managers who are skilled in effectively managing incredible ambiguity. A more spirited, educated, independent, self-reliant, health-conscious work force must be reckoned with.

We encourage you not to sidestep the painstaking effort required to create the core capabilities necessary to achieve sustainable productivity and employee involvement in a turbulent and rapidly changing marketplace. We hope you'll own up to the magnitude of the task. Change means disruption. It involves repatterning. It brings unknown challenges. Risks. Assaults on managerial egos. It devours outdated procedures. Submarines timidity and indecisiveness. Chisels away at proven track records. Forces growth.

These *toe-in-the water* prescriptions are designed to make you more comfortable with change. We hope you'll consider them useful.

---

40. Construct a best/worst scenario

Decisions, decisions, decisions! So often it's difficult to decide which course of action to take. We find that decision making becomes particularly difficult when the fear factor enters the picture. You know what we're talking about: fear of failure, fear of the unknown, fear of looking foolish, fear of making mistakes. This technique challenges you to take a stand—step out and make that decision, then go for it with confidence. Here's how it works.

Clearly describe the action you want to take, but feel powerless to do so. For example, we've seen managers struggle with public speaking, hiring or firing an employee, reorganizing a department, making cold calls, handling a complaint, questioning a policy, and so on. Be very specific in identifying what you want to do. Now, close your eyes and see yourself doing it. That's called faking it till you make it. What is the worst thing that could happen? Plunge headlong into the fantasy and visualize all the things that could turn sour if you were to do this particular thing. Take mental notes.

Then, relax a moment. Now ask yourself: "What is the best that can happen if I do it?" Again, get into the fantasy and really enjoy all the positive benefits. See a successful outcome. Jot down your thoughts.

Now, launch a reality check. Look at your "worst" fantasy and ask yourself: "What are the chances that any of this will happen?" Do the same for your "best" fantasy. We've found that, typically, the chances are much higher that the best fantasy will occur. By confronting your worst fears, you are able to put them in perspective and deal with them. So get ready to stretch to new professional heights as you release your potential and reach for the best you can be!

41. Examine the depth of your commitment

List twenty-five personal behaviors that demonstrate how much you care about your company because they convey genuine interest, respect, and care beyond lip service or hip-pocket interest. Examine your loyalty, above-and-beyond-the-call-of-duty commitment, work ethics, professional image, innovations and quality improvement suggestions, crusades, zeal, work relationships, bone-deep beliefs. What kind of corporate citizen are you? Consider your minute-to-minute behavior, and your language. How do you describe your company? Examine the depth of your commitment.

Ferret out twenty-five behaviors that show indifference (intended or otherwise) and transgressions that have tarnished your professional image (if only in your own mind). In what ways have you shown your insensitivity, dampened your own or someone else's enthusiasm, reneged on a promise, compromised quality, reinforced turf boundaries, cast undue criticism, protected the guilty, crucified the innocent, broken your promise? Examine the depth and breadth of your transgressions.

Place the positive behaviors you have listed in an envelope and tuck it in your desk drawer. Refer to it during one of those days when you need a lift in spirit. Select five of the most irresponsible transgressions and list them on a three-by-five card entitled "Crimes and Misdemeanors."

Take a good look at 'em. Now seal them in an envelope labeled "Checkup from the Neck Up" and date it six months from today. Promise yourself to eliminate each of these misdemeanors within six months. Monitor your behavior. At the designated time, reopen the envelope and evaluate your progress. If you've kicked the habit, cross out the negative behavior. If not, list the remaining *indictments* on another index card entitled "High Crimes and Self-Demeanors." Seal the card in a new envelope and date it six months hence. Repeat the process until you have eliminated each of the remaining transgressions.

The issues here are self-respect, integrity, self-renewal, honesty. In the end, your minute-to-minute actions provide a living model of excellence or insolence.

42. Be a knight in shining armor

Sit down with a stalled project team. Listen to them—for a full day perhaps. Ask questions. Probe. Interview. Organize a small quick-hit team of results-oriented doers and commit yourselves to breaking the logjam. Manage this bootleg operation. If you want to be involved in something that will give you some kicks, this is it. Bringing something that's dying back to life is invigorating. It's revitalizing. It's empowering. We're not fans of sloppy or shoddy work, so give this ad hoc adventure your best. This type of repair work is an inherently messy process. Egos are sensitive. Some perceptions from critics might take the form of "Who do you think you are anyway—a knight in shining armor?" "What gives you the right—to intrude—to meddle, uninvited—to throw your professonal weight around?"

As you no doubt recognize by now, we love interesting experiments—ones that put your professional credibility on the line. Puzzle over this project. Visualize a solution. Cultivate a bias for action. Do something. Start some kind of resuscitation scheme. Anything to gear up momentum. The longer the project sits, the more energy it'll take to get it moving again.

Monitor your progress. Take copious notes. Stick your professional neck out. Create waves. Practice purposeful impatience. Introduce solutions. Discuss your investigative, planning, and implementation strategies with doers.

43. Consult your crystal ball

Purposefully and systematically meet with junior people to discuss current and future trends in your industry. Will the services you provide and the products you sell be in demand five years from now? What type of competitive position will you enjoy, say, one year from now? Three? How about ten years from now? To what extent do you standardize—or customize—your services or products? What strategies will work in this high-tech/high-touch business culture?

Discuss the impact and relevance of such corporate realities as decentralization, targeted innovation, deregulation, bureaucracy, telecommunications linkages, paperless offices, cafeteria-style benefits systems, human capital as a strategic resource, the shift from an industrial to an information society, the entrepreneurial intrapreneurial revolutions, intuition and imagination as critical leadership skills, self-managed work teams. Other issues include global markets, autonomous divisions, shift from man-ager to order taker and from giver to facilitator, cheerleader and mentor, high-tech/high-touch, hired labor versus contract labor, proximity to market, direct mail, quality of work life, corporate needs versus employee values, unskilled versus poorly edu-cated people, and many more.

Determine how this globalized thinking relates to what you do and how you manage. The boundaries may seem blurred. These larger patterns are not always clear. This activity calls for a synthesis in an age of analysis. Its purpose is to provide a mechanism that helps forward-thinking managers gain global insights in a marketplace where complexity grows by quantum leaps and changes accelerate the demise of organizations too timid to take risks. Trends, like trains, are easier to ride in the direction they're headed. Several key concepts that will en-hance your trend-awareness abilities are recognition of similari-ties, sequences, processes, cycles, distributions, movements, shapes, tendencies, possibilities, probabilities, misalignments, and the like. The insights gained from these relationships can be explosive. Enlightening. Sobering. Overwhelming. Positively stimulating. Revitalizing.

44. Put your finger on the corporate pulse

Review your calendar for the past year. Examine the last ninety days in more detail. What does it tell you about what you con-sidered to be your substantive priorities, your involvement pro-clivities, your networking habits, your administrative activities, the company you keep, your planning ability, your high visibil-ity activities, your obsessive behaviors, mandatory activities, broken appointments, interruptions, office time versus field vis-its, and so on?

Are you focused on "cop tasks" or are you involved in managing for change? What process do you employ for managing change and ambiguity? Do you have one? How do you keep your finger on the corporate pulse? Whom do you define as a colleague? Determine the gap between what you scheduled and what you actually accomplished. How do you spend 80 percent of your time? Where? With whom? What activities can be combined? Delegated? Eliminated? How routinized is your workday? How many dividends (emotional, intellectual, physical) do you enjoy at the end of your workday? What habits have you found? Check for addictions, too. You've probably got a couple of them—you know, like procrastinating, overanalyzing, staring (zombielike) into space, hiding behind your desk, engaging in trivial pursuits. To what degree is your current way of doing business satisfying and productive?

Based on an honest and thoughtful analysis of each of the questions above, begin to make improvements in the way you manage work. Take small steps. Incrementalize improvement. Celebrate each small win. Use sensible approximation—the price of perfection is prohibitive. We're reminded of the old saw: "Good judgment is the product of experience; experience is the product of bad judgment." This retrospective check allows you midcourse corrections. However, don't throw the baby out with the bath water. Continue doing what you do well. Modify or eliminate nonproductive behavior. Otherwise, you'll be overcooked and underfed.

45. Unzip your resistance

Flexibility, a willingness to manage chaos, a healthy acceptance of ambiguity, and an uncanny ability to manage multiple priorities are key prerequisites for dealing effectively with rapidly changing corporate realities. The pace of accelerated change is phenomenal. Managerial elasticity and recuperative powers for shepherding people and launching services and products through leaky systems and hard times are at an all-time high. Competition is fierce. Stakes are high. Hundreds of managers (or is it thousands?) have been derailed and subsequently assigned to the scrap heap because they failed to accept the inevitability of change. Prying some managers loose from prehistoric beliefs, frozen (unyielding, cemented) attitudes, and outdated assumptions takes considerable managerial torque. Some antediluvian beliefs will have to be dynamited out! One thing is for certain— any manager who fails to or refuses to change will suffer inexorably and face unrelenting horrors in the years to come, both personally and professionally. (Do we have your attention? We hope so!)

Our prescription for healthy, productive, and decisive leadership: Untie your Gordian knot. Loosen up. Welcome change. Unzip your resistance. Climb out of your self-imposed rut (quickly, we might add). However, once you're out of the rut, proceed slowly. Deliberately. Intentionally. Faithfully. Begin by designing an incremental change program. When? Now, of course! Immediately. Where? Everywhere. Personally and professionally. In every area of your life. What does the program consist of? Positive change. Small step self-exploration opportunities. Minuscule course corrections. Major turns. Inner child calisthenics. Self-renewal. Tantalizing fun. Emotional tenderizing. Intellectual aerobics. Spiritual deepening. Physical agility.

Here are some of our favorite calisthenics for change strategies: Brush your teeth (comb your hair, button your shirt or blouse) with your nondominant hand; enroll in a drama class; drive home a different way; adopt a new hobby that seems totally uncharacteristic of you; walk around the house barefooted; snuggle up to a potter's wheel and mold clay; enjoy an afternoon snooze in the hammock; if you like fried eggs, scramble 'em; if you're partial to red meat, go vegetarian for a day; within a reasonable time span, eliminate an old, entrenched habit; refrain from wearing your watch for a couple of days; fast for a day; write your name (in cursive) and draw a picture with your nondominant hand; walk barefooted in a creek or stream; stand in the longest line at the supermarket; rechannel your gamesmanship energies and play to lose (at least some of the time); give one of your material possessions away to someone who will appreciate the gesture; avoid watching the news for a day; do something you haven't ever done before (like complimenting your mother-in-law or remembering your wedding anniversary); get to work an hour earlier than usual; back into a parking place instead of pulling in; turn back the brightness knob and listen to TV instead of watching it; draw two pictures simultaneously, using both hands; take all the chairs out of the conference room and then hold the meeting; eat dinner by feeding yourself with the wrong hand; take a brisk walk or swim during lunch instead of dining out; at the next tollbooth you encounter on an important trip, give the attendant enough fare to cover the vehicle behind you as well; enjoy a complete body massage; talk to marketing, manufacturing, sales, or accounting people; eat tofu; drink a large glass of grapefruit juice; sail; parachute or skydive; change your hair style; if you have a fetish for murder mysteries, read biographies or autobiographies; adopt a new craft or hobby; complete each of the other one hundred ways to bypass training. (Go ahead—we'll write more.)

Communicating for Results

It is no exaggeration to say that effective communication is a necessary condition for service distinctiveness and sustained productivity. It is absolutely fundamental. The connection between appropriate communication, communication competence, productive and satisfying interpersonal relations, and motivating people is real and thematic throughout each of the 101 prescriptions outlined in this management development book. The prescriptions in this section serve as learning laboratories to help enhance your ability to truly communicate. To identify how the interplay between environments, circumstances, and people affects every communication exchange.

Enhancing your repertoire of interpersonal communication skills is our aim. These activities will complement classroom training by providing you real-world opportunities to practice a variety of communication skills. Skill improvement areas include feedback and disclosure skills. Initiating and maintaining a smooth flow of mutually satisfying information exchange. Empathy. Nonverbal gestures that legitimize what you say. Conversational relaxation. Attentive listening. Conflict resolution. Public speaking. Presentation skills.

In the give and take of a communication transaction, each conversationalist is responsible for ensuring open and free exchange of ideas. When you communicate, people's feelings and well-being are within your influence. You can build relationships with well-timed and compassionate dialogue. Relationships can be destroyed in an instant by a singularly misplaced gesture or demeaning comment. You will never escape that fact.

Communicating to ensure legendary service and product quality is your professional responsibility. Communicating to move people to outperform themselves is your managerial duty. A communication climate that spawns gut-level honesty, integrity, openness, and care is your high calling as a leader of people.

46. Capture thoughts in your Writer's Digest

In an easy-to-reach desk drawer, store a logbook to capture examples of clever phrases, styles of writing, action verbs, unique performance wording, industry-specific terminology, quotable quotes, and the like. The idea is to establish a writer's digest as a resource to improve your written communications. We're asking you to move beyond the traditional (and boring) expository style of report writing to a more persuasive style.

Why? We believe that all business *is* show business. We extend that perspective to management as well—all leadership *is* show business. In our experience we find that given a little direction, a few resources, and a touch of the dramatic, people will drive themselves to unbelievable excellence. Persuasive communication, whether written or spoken, will continue to be one of the key leadership skills. A letter well written or a speech well delivered moves people. Emotional appeal moves people. We subscribe to Tom Peters' descriptions of a leader versus a manager. Peters prophesies:

> For the last twenty-five years we have carried around with us the model of Manager as cop, referee, devil's advocate, dispassionate analyst, professional, decision-maker, naysayer, pronouncer. This alternative we now propose is leader (not manager) as cheerleader, enthusiast, nurturer of champions, hero-finder, wanderer, drama-tist, coach, facilitator, builder.
>
> Peters, Tom. *Thriving on Chaos*, New York: Alfred A. Knopf, 1987.

Given the new trappings of leadership, is it any wonder that persuasive, not evasive, communication is called for? This is your opportunity to catalog powerful communication technology. You'll want to include phrases that help you communicate your passion, care, unfailing commitment, and unshakable belief in what you do for a living. To help you get started we've included a few notes from our Writer's Digest (Exhibit 9). We are frequently asked if managers actually do this, actually go to the trouble of recording power words. Our enthusiastic reply is,

"You bet your Cross pen they do." We hasten to add that the price of leadership excellence is time and energy. Occasionally the very same time and energy that could have gone toward enjoying your son's or daughter's class play or gymnastics competition will have to be devoted to a pressing business need. When you are truly committed to doing what it takes to evolve into an exceptional leader, you'll stand taller. You'll admit to the struggle, but you'll also have squarely and solidly placed a smile on your face that just won't quit.

47. Pick a hot topic

Select one communication skill you want to focus on for a month (clarifying expectations, positive feedback, managing disagreement, horizontal delegation, coaching or counseling, or something else). Set weekly self-measurement goals. Realize that you *are* your enacted priorities. Live with the specific communication behavior you want to improve. Go to meetings with it. Visit work sites with it. Shower with it. Sleep with it. The art is to bring this one simple communication skill to life. Immerse yourself in it. Experiment. Jot down each occasion, each circumstance, that required you to use the targeted communication behavior. Gauge your progress. Describe how you demonstrated the use of the skill. Force yourself to use the communication behavior as often as possible (inside or outside of work) during the next thirty days. Take this opportunity to make this a self-education opportunity in-progress. We have provided two self-assessment tools to help get you started: the Communication Competence Checklist (Exhibit 10), and the Interpersonal Encounter Expectations Check (Exhibit 11). Use these to heighten your sensitivity and awareness in monitoring your communication behaviors. If the spirit moves you, construct an instrument of your own to focus on your hot topic.

48. Conduct a language audit

Personally conduct a language audit. Listen attentively to what people say. How are employees, supervisors, managers, customers, and the company itself referred to? What labels and descriptors are assigned to company executives? In what ways does the language you hear show pride in the company, its services, its products, its mission, its markets? In what ways is the language complimentary? Derogatory? Positive? Less than encouraging? Does the conversation foul the air? Is the tone of the language laced with thinly disguised contempt? Or is it spiced with loyalty, commitment, and pride? (We must remind you, none too gently, that one of the biggest barriers to sustainable superior performance is contempt for the customer and contempt for co-workers.) How often do you hear genuine, not phony, involvement expressed? How are co-workers at all levels viewed? Is the talk focused on personality differences, turf issues, yesterday's sports scores, or outside interests? Or do you hear echoes of enthusiastic chatter about revenue line enhancement, quality, customer-obsession, market orientation, profitability, competitive positioning, and the like?

One thing is certain. When we consider the nature of an organization, its leadership, and the growing trends of decentralization, complexity, global markets, and employee involvement, we are drawn to the following conclusion: Today's organization requires crystal-clear communication, the utmost integrity, and unmitigated openness at all levels. Chief among the demands made on organizations is the increasing necessity for a communication climate compatible with the psychic needs of the organization's members. The earliest indicators of a misalignment between organizational goals and employee values are the type, quality, and direction of the language spoken in the shops, the offices, and the boardrooms.

Spend a solid week quietly (and unconfrontationally) listening to the organizational chatter. Take mental notes. Notice the patterns and trends that emerge. Record your thoughts. Make no judgments about what is said, who said it, or under what circumstances it is uttered. Consider the following questions: What is it about your organizational climate that perpetuates such dialogue? In what ways is the language characteristic of the attitudes felt toward management, support staff, hourly employees, and customers? What element of the language excites you, encourages you, makes you proud to be a key contributor in your organization's success? Does the language that echoes down the corporate hallways upset you in any way? Does it fill you with a sense of pride?

What will you do now with the results of this audit? What responsibility do you have in cultivating an atmosphere of trust, cooperation, respect, dignity, loyalty, commitment, integrity? How will you clean up your air? Chat with your manager? Agree to take better care of your people? How will you relieve sources of *atmospheric pressure*? Change their hearts, and you'll change their language.

49. Pay tough-minded respect

Draft a people philosophy bill of rights, suitable for sitewide posting. For the sake of your career, we strongly urge you to refrain from making this a declaration based on lip service or facade. Before you tackle this developmental option, make sure your beliefs in the goodness and uniqueness and priceless value of people and *love* (yes, we include that four-letter word here in a management development book, of all things) for them are ingrained bone deep. Draft a bill of rights that says in effect that the management of this organization believes that we must treat people with respect; make people winners, not whiners; let them stand out; treat them with dignity; trust them; forgive them; empower them. You must believe in this—unequivocally and without reservation.

Permit us to make one more point. We are not talking about mollycoddling, spoiling, or overpatronizing the troops. We are talking about tough-minded respect and admiration for people and the willingness to provide the developmental scaffolding to help ordinary people achieve extraordinary results.

After you draft your version of the bill of rights, ask colleagues to do the same. Compare. Integrate. Compile. Fine-tune. Polish exquisitely. Publish proudly. Honor unfailingly.

50. When push comes to shove, legitimize it

One of the key skills for managers who want to remain productive and responsive to performance improvement is that of managing disagreement and conflict. Recognized and accepted for what it is, conflict can be tolerated and creatively channeled or resolved for effective group performance. This activity helps you identify your *conflict style.*

Conflict occurs when two or more people attempt to occupy the same space at the same time. This space can be physical, psychological, or emotional when perceptions, beliefs, and values differ. No matter what the setting, conflict is inevitable since people have different viewpoints. People carry these personal perceptions into the workplace and view the needs of the organization differently.

Since conflict is natural, your goal is to minimize or eliminate dysfunctional disagreements and seek constructive resolutions. Everyone must be involved in order to reduce the breeding ground of conflict. Solutions reached through shared responsibility are usually much more acceptable and pragmatic than those imposed from above.

Before we continue, one extremely important point should be made. Conflict can be healthy. Conflict is a natural part of work life. Dealing with confrontation creatively can strengthen rather than destroy work relationships. The purpose of the When Push Comes to Shove activity is to help you see the healthy aspects of conflict, thereby stripping it of its mystical qualities. Legitimizing conflict is essential for group development. One of

the most valuable skills in handling or resolving conflict issues
is the art of *creative fighting*. Clearing the air and getting disagreements out in the open can help groups come to terms with
long-standing aliments. The important consideration is to
process the conflict effectively and efficiently.

Whether the outcome of the conflict issue is positive or negative is almost totally determined by the way it is managed. Some
conflict issues are more easily managed than others. The ability
to successfully manage conflict is one of the most important
social skills work groups can develop. We categorize conflict
into five major styles. Most managers adopt certain preferred
ways of dealing with conflict. Unfortunately, too many managers
operate out of one preferred conflict style. Each of us has access
to several conflict management styles, but we tend to use one or
two styles and exclude other styles that could be more effective
in a given situation.

Adjourn to the privacy of your home or office and turn to
Conflict Styles Questionnaire (Exhibit 12). Complete the self-
assessment instrument and scoring sheet. Then answer the professional development questions in Assessing Your Conflict
Management Styles (Exhibit 13). Review the descriptions of
each of the five styles described on Conflict Management Styles
(Exhibit 14) and identify your proclivities for managing disagreement.

The fundamental purpose of this developmental activity is to
remind you to move through the corporate hallways and cor-
ridors with power and grace. It's about choosing to remain calm
and centered in any storm. To act with dignity and elegance in
the midst of anger and chaos. To walk confidently—and compas-
sionately—through emotional battlefields.

We believe you are a gem in the rough, however gritty and
rigid you sometimes appear to be. The insults and assaults that
occasionally appear are the sandpaper we need to smooth out
these rough edges. The gift of assuming managerial responsibility is that you are able to participate consciously and deliberately in this organizational smoothing by helping those concerned achieve balance. Direction. Perspective. And renewed
commitment toward the common good.

51. Put acronyms to good use

The world is being overtaken by acronyms! Acronym: A series of letters that represent a longer, more involved phrase. In fact, some of the most popular acronyms have become accepted words: radar, TV, fax.

We have noticed that acronymania is particularly rampant in organizations. Recently we were baffled by an acronym used by one of our clients, and asked what it stood for. Guess what? No one knew! (The acronym was SATYOP.) Business and industry's love affair with acronyms means they're here to stay. So let's put 'em to good use. We thought we'd include two in this prescription to challenge you to bypass standard operating procedures (SOPs) and try these ASAP!

1. DBMP-BMS—This delightful acronym relates to a problem experienced by many supervisors and managers. How many times have you delegated a project, only to have it boomerang from a colleague or subordinate who abdicates responsibility? Too often managers allow subordinates to play this ricochet game. It's nonproductive. It's a time robber. It's an abomination. It's positively offensive. It's a prime candidate for DBMP-BMS.

   Use DBMP-BMS. It is a philosophy of management that translates to Don't Bring Me Problems, Bring Me Solutions. When problems delegated by you are boomeranged back at you, refuse to take them! Ask the indecisive colleague: "How do you suggest we handle that?" or "What ideas do you have to deal with this problem?"

2. KISS—Despite first impressions, this technique does not advocate sexual advances! It just reminds you to monitor your communication with employees, and to Keep It Short and Simple. Don't strangle your language (verbal or written) with seventy-five-cent words and involved technical descriptions. Review recent memos you've written and identify any ways you could have simplified them.

Practice giving directions to employees and verify that
they are clear and understandable. Apply the KISS technique, and everyone will love you.

52. Publish or perish

Write an article on some area of leadership development. The
article should be 2,500 to 4,000 words in length, typed (error-
free), and written on a subject you care about. Are passionate
about. Are proud of—exceedingly. Have no qualms writing
about.

Whether you consider yourself a writer or not, we encourage
you to ask someone you respect to edit your manuscript. We
would prefer your *not* using an expository style of business
writing. Instead use a more fluid, open, and persuasive style.
Write the way you talk. Be creative. Forceful. Anoint those who
read it with substance and applicability. Stimulate the reader.
Immortalize a management principle. Enshrine a people philosophy and service or product quality bias (only if you honestly
believe they're important and have demonstrated your belief in
people, service excellence, and uncompromised product quality). Deputize those readers who share your passion for excellence. Detonate company pride. Emboss your penchant for unfailing commitment on every heart. Hoist a key management
concept for all to see. Toast teamwork or distinctive customer
service or interdepartmental cooperation. Rattle a few cages.
Knock down any remnants of turfism. Unstop communication
bottlenecks. Punctuate top management's willingness to take
care of its people.

Now, sell your next level of management on the idea of
replicating this scholarly assignment companywide. Create your
own industry-specific trade publication. Chair the start-up committee to organize an annual Management Bulletin composed of
articles submitted by colleagues. Publish these journal articles

organizationwide. Rotate the chairperson each year. Use this opportunity to invite submissions from managers at all levels. Make it a big deal. Accept only well-written entries from committed managers. Spawn insights from as many functional areas as possible. Rekindle esprit de corps. Cultivate oneness and unity.

Distribute copies of the Management Bulletin to all employees each year. Spread the word. Radiate the management philosophy. Blitz the troops with messages from managers they admire and respect.

We have seen this kind of publication galvanize an industry. Without a clearly articulated management philosophy, a strong and legitimate management presence, and an honestly run care-and-feeding-of-people orientation, industries fail. They slowly perish. They even vanish. So put the word out. Publish or perish.

53. Polish your speaking skills

Write a five- to seven-minute speech on an area of your professional specialty. In the privacy of your home or office, rehearse the speech until you know it by heart. Practice speaking in front of a mirror after you have memorized your speech. Make each presentation a dress rehearsal—outfit yourself in your business suit. Speak passionately. Forcefully. Confidently. Do whatever you have to do to organize your speech. Join the local Toastmasters. Contract the services of a speaking professional. Enroll in a presentation skills training class. Watch professional speakers, public officials, the clergy, and so forth. Acquire a speaking personality. Captivate your imaginary audience. Fake it till you make it, in your mind's eye, by visualizing yourself delivering exceptional speeches.

Once you feel polished, confident, and just plain pleased with your progress, videotape your speech. (Prerequisites: Do not videotape your speech until you have delivered the same speech at least twenty-five times—we're serious. At least twenty-five times!) Even with the fine-tuning, you'll find that the quality of your presentation skills will improve with dedicated practice. Apply what you've learned at Toastmasters meetings or from private tutoring or in classroom settings. Schedule opportunities to speak at local clubs and associations. Use this same speech. The idea is to make this one speech as informative and as professional as possible. Six months from the date you videotaped the first speech, videotape the new and much improved version (we hope). Compare the two speeches. In what ways have you improved? Which are your more polished platform skills? Define your presentation style. Evaluate your mannerisms. List areas of improvement. Sharpen your platform skills. Gauge your progress.

Repeat the process using new material. Rehearse the new five- to seven-minute speech. Stand poised and ready in front of a mirror. Practice the speech until you feel satisfied that is has been consummately delivered. Deliver it proudly for at least twenty-five satisfying performances in front of a mirror. Videotape your speech again. Compare it to your first tape. Analyze it. Dissect it. Admire your progress. Catalogue areas of improvement. Toast your success.

Use these videotaped speeches as developmental tools. The issue: All of the rigorous research, every inch of technical knowledge and skill, each well thought-out plan, can collect dust on the floor of almost-made-its if the way it is presented to management stinks. Presentation skills are extremely important. Delivery is everything! Selling your service, product, new plan or idea (no matter how well researched, organized, innovative, beneficial, or profitable) depends on your ability to convince your audience of its merit. Technically speaking, the well-prepared, well-delivered speech or presentation gets results. A poorly prepared, extremely well-delivered presentation will even get favorable results. However, we have seen (far too many times) an extremely well-prepared report or request fall on deaf (and bored and totally unreceptive) ears because the manager's delivery skills stunk. As resource allocations and funding options become even more scarce, the manager who personifies the *total package* will enjoy unprecedented success in gaining the approvals he or she needs to meet and exceed corporate goals.

===

54. Thrill newcomers with a video hello

Produce a slide-tape or video presentation as part of a new employee orientation for your divison, department, or plant site. Decide how you want to represent the company. What image do you want to project to new hires? How do you want them to see the company? Present a big picture. Organizational values. People philosophy. Mission. As director, producer, and writer, you may also want to consider including a brief history of the company. If you have a corporate communciations division, you'll want to work closely with a video production specialist. This project will require interdivisional interfaces to gather the input necessary to write the script, should you decide to develop an organizationwide orientation package. One that's motivational and upbeat. (Remember who the audience is.) Consider how to plan for updates and revisions without duplication of effort.

It'll take all the communicative and investigative skills you have to form concise snapshots of each functional area's role and responsibilities. Plan to include a message from the site manager or division head (depending upon the scope of the project). Don't hesitate to be creative. Get other people involved. Deputize. Delegate. Recruit.

Plan to produce an engaging piece. Paint a positive picture. An accurate portrayal. Reaffirm, in the new hire's mind, that this is a great place to work. Instill pride. And uncompromised quality. Preach obsessively responsive service. Praise employee involvement. Thrill the newcomer with visions of reciprocal growth and mutually satisfying opportunities for lasting prosperity. Advertise only what you can deliver. Read that last statement again. One more time. Why? Because expectations are built here. Buy-in starts here. The alignment between corporate promises and actions is suggested here. Credibility is punctuated here.

55. Add sign language to your communication repertoire

Strive more valiantly than ever to epitomize the great communicator by eliminating all conceivable obstacles to communicating effectively. We have suggested prescriptions and improvement of more traditional communication competencies, such as attentive listening, giving and receiving feedback, written communications, nonverbal communication, and so forth. The focus of this prescription is sign language.

We strongly recommend your not taking this opportunity lightly. Enhancing the repertoire of the range and quality of your interpersonal communication skills is vital for productive and rewarding interpersonal living. Increasing the size and variety of your communication expertise can provide the leverage you need to handle unique communication opportunities, particularly when alternatives to traditional dialogue are called for. Learning sign language is another important step in legitimizing your true concern for individual differences and human relationships. It shows your sensitivity for the special communication needs of the physically challenged. More and more organizations are benefiting from the employment of physically challenged persons. Hiring of the handicapped is on the rise. The opportunities for you to become involved professionally with a physically challenged colleague are higher today than even five years ago.

Obviously, knowing how to sign will increase your ability to initiate and maintain a smooth flow of mutual exchange, feel at ease and comfortable during the conversational encounter, and fortify the mutual respect such a relationship bond produces between two people. Bashing language and communication barriers is a high management calling. Take responsibility for meeting someone on his or her communication level. Be a basher of communication barriers. Adopt signing as your second language.

You'll find hundreds of ingenious applications for your new language. Communicating at a distance (across a crowded lunch room—or stuffy conference room—or noisy shop area) is considerably easier, and more efficient and less conspicuous than shouting. Close-quartered elevators prove no obstacle for carrying on a private conversation. Use signing to break the monotony of daylong staff meetings by sending messages to well-versed colleagues. Well-timed humor is delightful, too. Carry on important conversations as you walk down busy corporate hallways. Enjoy your new language. Strike up conversations with a hearing-impaired colleague or customer.

You can start by attending a basic sign language course at a local high school, college, or university. Religious organizations also offer signing classes as part of their outreach focus. Books are available at libraries or bookstores. So speak volumes—learn to speak the silent language.

===

56. Build overseas connections

Whether you're ready or not, the global village has arrived. Like it or not, you're a participant in a single global market. The explosion of products and technology has brought international competition to your doorstep. This prescription, though broadly concerned with internationalism, recognizes action in two particular areas: international relationship development and foreign language competence. World peace through world trade and international cooperation and goodwill is the focus of this *developmental ramp*. We're strong believers in it. Offshore markets and overseas friends are two solidly entrenched goals in our strategic plan.

Master relationship building and learn the culture in at least two overseas countries. Do this within the next two years. By definition, this globalized cross-cultural education begins with the basic language skills development. We recommend several languages as excellent starting points: German, Japanese, Chinese, and Russian.

Join internationally focused organizations such as the Friendship Force, the Center for International Understanding, the World Center, and Citizens for Understanding International Exchange. Attend international festivals in your locale. Contact local colleges and universities and ask for information about international studies and exchange programs. Both Duke University (Durham, NC) and Brigham Young University (Salt Lake City, UT) have catalogs that offer cultural descriptions and analyses of more than 120 countries through their International Studies Departments. Tour English-speaking countries first; than expand your travels to any other interesting place on the planet. Take advantage of any opportunity to become a global citizen—and friend.

57. Spruce up your information systems savvy

This prescription is designed to help you—the end user—to become more sophisticated in assessing your data processing (DP) and integration needs and in identifying what you want in software applications suitability. Many managers, unhappy with off-the-shelf IS (information systems) packages from vendors, leverage their expertise by developing alliances with in-house DP analysts and programmers. Select an existing generic DP program, and have the program customized to meet their specific IS needs. You can do the same!

Collaborate to develop new packages for crucial foundational systems. Create functionally rich information systems faster and more economically. More reliably—and with due consideration given to existing architecture (PCs and minis). Enter into these development ventures with a sense of partnership. Camaraderie. Trust. Roll-up-your-sleeves commitment.

Keep the scope small enough to be manageable, yet broad enough to be of interest. Don't limit yourself to automating the processing of data in clerical, accounting, or number-crunching applications. Target professional-level decision and planning tasks that require the manipulation of symbols (knowledge and conceptual relationships).

Work with DP personnel eyeball to eyeball. Shoulder to shoulder. Loosen your tie. Unzip your assumptions—keeping complex systems running is extremely difficult. (Most managers outside the DP department fail to fully understand that.) Work closely with programmers. Systems analysts. Lead applications programmers. Data-base administrators. Develop genuine professional relationships with the Director of DP/MIS of the Information Center Manager in your organization.

Learn information systems terminology. Know what real-time data collection means. Add these terms to your managerial communication repertoire: batch, batch-oriented, batch updates, disk drive, data base, modem, trend analysis, integrate the files, security strategy, proprietary programming, workstation-controlled networks, laptop computer, on-line, disk-space, RAM disk technology, peripheral parts, multivendor connectivity, antivirus resources, migration tools, machine dependency, bar code reader.

Our hope is that you'll become empowered by education and experience. That you'll begin to appreciate the *dentistry* and mind-reading talents of DP analysts and programmers as they attempt to pull relevant information "teeth" from users. We see the need for an integration of DP personnel as partners with users to shepherd the knowledgeable user through the pains and perils of developing modifications and upgrades to information systems that are relevant and sustainable. Plan to spend ten to twenty hours on a mini-DP project. See it through.

58. Add a penny for your positive thoughts

We hear it all the time: "Oh, yeah, I compliment my people!" or "Sure, I tell my employees when they do it right." Most supervisors truly believe they provide positive feedback, but our research confirms the opposite. People are told (and told and told) when they do something wrong, but when they do it right—the sounds of silence are deafening.

It's important to become aware of how often you give positive reinforcement to your employees. Why? People will repeat behavior they are rewarded for. Read that last sentence one more time—it's true! (We promise.) So, reward behavior you want to see repeated.

This strategy will help build your awareness of how often you identify and reinforce positive behavior. First thing in the morning, put a handful of pennies in your pocket. Every time you provide positive, specific feedback to an employee, transfer a penny to a pocket on the other side. (Warning: Don't be so obvious that employees see you do this. They'll want the penny!)

The goal, obviously, is to transfer all the pennies from one pocket to the other. The benefit is that you become acutely aware of how generous or meager you are with compliments.

59. Adopt byte-sized projects

Since the turn of the century, only a handful of significant technological developments have directly affected the everyday lives of all of us—the electric light bulb, telephone, automobile, radio, television, moving pictures, telecommunications satellites, nuclear energy, and most recently, the electronic digital computer. Breakthroughs in computer technology have made personal computers accessible.

One of the chief communications and organizational skills for managers today is computer literacy. Advances in information technology will mean little unless users of new systems and software apply such tools to their managerial repertoire. We encourage you to take a fresh (and sober) look at computer literacy skills.

Most organizational changes you'll see in your professional lifetime will be part of a general shift toward networking—a transition that is now reflected in most salary and compensation structures that reward results via telecommunications and data management skills. Connectivity through skill in using multiple communications protocols is a key management decision-making imperative. PCs and work stations are everywhere, patronized by users who howl for mainframe access. Local area networks are also on the rise. Whether your operational needs require a hierarchical, mainframe-controlled network or organizationwide network management from intelligent work stations, you'll have to be a knowledgeable and savvy end user yourself.

One of the organizational realities managers now face is that computer literacy is a must. Do not allow yourself to be intimidated by the computer mystique. Use this exquisite piece of communications technology to gain your productivity and operational advantage. This byte-sized prescription asks you to reach out and touch a computer (PC or laptop). Introduce yourself. Get to know each other. Develop an ongoing relationship. Talk to each other. Connect. Substitute your hard head for a hard disk.

Managing Time

In this age of rapid change, unyielding marketplace demands, and phenomenal access to information, more and more managers feel they are squeezed by time—and pulverized by multiple priorities. Time is money. Time is how we measure life and the workday. It is irreversible. Irreplaceable. It moves inexorably through your coffee break and past project implementation dates. That's what time does best—fly when you're having fun and crawl when you're attending one of those board meetings.

Each of the following prescriptions goes beyond most superficial time management techniques, hoists you above time constraints, and annihilates bothersome time robbers. We think you'll agree that one of the mammoth payoffs in achieving greater control of your time is greater control over your life. So it just makes good business sense to manage time effectively. We're convinced that mediocrity is self-inflicted, that procrastination is a matter of choice, and that staring out the window or at the overloaded desk top is habit. We're just as convinced that you can do something about it. We think these few prescriptions can help.

We invite you to be a basher of time barriers. Practice our ABCs. Transistorize your time robbers. Avoid the unplanned-event treadmill. Vaporize waiting time. Immortalize your wastebasket. Muzzle interrupters. And have the time of your life.

60. Divert the paper avalanche

Select from one to four first-line management, staff, or critical support personnel jobs. Collect as much information as possible on "how it *feels* to work there day after day," with a focus on the paperwork handled. To get this information, use anonymous questionnaires, individual or group interviews, reports, meetings, written communication, procedures statements. Pay particular attention to the volume, type, and source of the paper avalanche. Then spend two full days performing the job. (That may mean changing your eating habits, rescheduling Spa workouts, or postponing Wednesday night's card game. We never promised you a rose garden. But you'll no doubt uncover some thorny issues related to the amount of unnecessary paperwork involved in day-to-day operations.) Ask three or four colleagues in your department to do the same thing. Think they'll gain similar insights? You bet! Now spend one or two days, preferably off site, to compare notes. Agree to take immediate action as a group, to cut paperwork by twenty percent, then by thirty percent within a month. Gather around the recycling bin or the paper shredder and show the troops the fruits of your diligent labors. If this is a serious enterprise (and we think it ought to be), discuss ways to prevent another paper avalanche.

This developmental event features a strong dose of what psychologists call the Hawthorne Effect (employees will improve their behavior simply because management is paying attention to them). The caution here is to realize the short-term benefits of diverting this paper avalanche and recognize that people (including yourself) fall into old patterns. We are suggesting a restructuring of the way you handle information—formally and informally. This task is not for the faint of heart.

61. Float through paperwork using the RAFT technique

The higher you climb the corporate ladder, the more paperwork you have to handle. The ability to manage the flood of paper that crosses your desk becomes a number-one priority! This developmental activity—the RAFT technique—will help you "float" through paperwork, and strengthen your time management skills.

Stack up all the paper on your desk. For each piece of paper, apply the RAFT formula:

R = Redirect It! This is a devious technique, but very effective. The point here is to get the paper off your desk and onto someone else's desk! Be creative! Use notes such as: For your information; Please handle; Thought you'd be interested in this; Why did I get this?; and the like.

A = Act on It! It has been estimated that approximately seven hours per week are wasted just moving paper on a desk. Get rid of it the first time you handle it. Use our philosophy: Every time you touch a piece of paper, move it one step closer to completion. (See the Dot Test, Prescription 63.)

F = File It! Don't add it to a stack to be filed. File it! This serves two purposes. It gets paper off your desk, and it familiarizes you with the files. If your files leave a lot to be desired, ask for a "Meet the Pro" session with someone who does it well. (See Prescription 25.)

T = Trash It! You could probably eliminate 50 percent or more of the paper on your desk and never miss the white rain. So go ahead—make your day. Say a fond farewell to those useless pieces of paper taking up space, and send them on to their next assignment.

62. Construct a procrastination profile

Do not put this technique off until tomorrow! Procrastination is a deadly habit, but it can be managed. We have found that most managers perpetuate a pattern that reflects their procrastination habit. After you identify the pattern, you can attack and overcome it!

We're asking you to be brutally honest with yourself. Until you recognize your delay tactics, you can't modify or eliminate nonproductive behavior. So get rid of all the facades and excuses. Take a good hard look at your procrastination profile.

Use the following guide to profile yourself:

1. *What types of projects or in what situations do you consistently procrastinate?* Statistical analyses, narrative reports, telephone calls, performance reviews, dealing with a specific department or person, exercise? If you have difficulty with this question, observe your habits for a week or two. Become acutely aware of when you are avoiding something, and write it down. Then, review the list. You'll find a pattern—we promise!

2. *Now that you're aware of the situations in which you procrastinate, become aware of what you do instead.* Chances are you're doing some low-priority task to avoid the big one—and chances are you've convinced yourself that what you're doing is important. We're great at rationalizing our behavior—but have you ever considered that "rationalize" means just that: "rational lies"? Identify your cover-up techniques. Again, there will probably be a pattern. Examples we've seen (and experienced, we must admit) include getting coffee (or other diversionary eating strategies); cleaning up desk, files, and so on; making phone calls; taking two-hour lunches; reviewing client files; rewriting material; attending unnecessary meetings (or calling them); photocopying reports (or cartoons); and the list goes on and on. The question is: What number-one priority are you avoiding by using these stall tactics?

3. So far you've identified your procrastination patterns. So we thought we'd put this third prescription off until now. (Just kidding!) *What rewards can you establish to motivate yourself to action?* The value of the reward can range from a collegiate-type star on your calendar to an afternoon on the golf course or tennis court. The only condition is that the reward must be totally and completely in your control to give to yourself. We've found it most effective to match the value of the reward with the degree of avoidance you are experiencing.

Now you've gathered the information. It is useful to chart it, using a format similar to the Procrastination Profile (Exhibit 15). Post it near your desk so that it's facing you. When you slip into your procrastination habit, you'll see it light up like a neon sign. The gentle reminder will seem to appear from nowhere. Take immediate action. Do it *now*!

63. Use the DOT test

This is a quick and easy developmental tool, but don't be fooled by its simplicity. It is a powerful prescription that can help you eliminate the time-robbing habit of circulating papers on your desk with nonproductive results by connecting the dots.

   Commit yourself to the diligent application of this technique for just two weeks and you'll be amazed at the number of red dots you'll encounter. For two weeks: every time you touch a piece of paper, for whatever reason, make a little red dot at the top. Here's the kicker: When you pick up a report or memo and notice it has thirty-seven dots on it, guess what? You've confused activity with accomplishment. You're guilty of moving paper unproductively on the merry-go-round called procrastination! Once you're aware that this unnecessary paper shuffle is an issue for you, use the White-Paper Rafting Technique (Prescription 61) to help you improve even more.

64. Clip and save

Do you find yourself buried under a mountain of magazines and professional journals? You know you need to read them. You recognize they're packed with important industry-specific information. You want to read them—someday. The very prospect seems overwhelming. They just continue to stack up, and sit there staring at you, creating feelings of guilt every time you see them.

This simple technique has many benefits. It will help you reduce Mt. Everest to a foothill. It will help keep you up-to-date on your reading. And it will provide you with a more productive use of "waiting time" (that dead time that is wasted when you are waiting for meetings to begin or for someone to arrive).

Retrieve a stapler, scissors, and highlighter. Open that first journal or magazine and scan the table of contents. Identify the articles of primary interest to you. Then clip those articles. (Hint: Be sure to get the entire article. Some articles are parceled out, with the last few paragraphs on obscure pages near the back.) Staple the article together and place it in the Reading File you just created. Discard the rest of the magazine! Get in the clip-and-save habit as soon as your magazines and journals arrive. Don't give them a chance to pile up.

Whenever you travel, there will be "down time," so slip your Reading File (or a few articles from it) into your attaché case. You'll never feel frustrated with wasted time again, and you'll stay current with the latest information from your journals.

Once you've read the article, make a decision to pass it on to someone else, file it, or toss it. If you decide to file it, be sure it's reference material you really need to keep. We challenge you to avoid saving articles "just in case you'll need to refer to them someday." If there are two or three key points you find useful, record them on a three-by-five card or log them in your computer and then toss or reroute the article.

65. Pass the buck

Delegation: the art of getting someone else to do the job! It's a critical leadership skill, but also one of the most misunderstood and misused. Are you one of those folks who believe "If you want a job done right, do it yourself"? Or perhaps you believe that by the time you tell someone else to do it, you could have done it yourself? The art of effective delegation isn't easy. In fact, it can be excruciatingly painful. But if you want to be a successful leader, you must feel comfortable empowering people. This technique will help you sharpen those delegation skills.

Evaluate the job to be delegated, and determine who is the best person to do it. Then select from the following levels of delegation dialogue the one most appropriate for the situation and the delegatee:

- Investigate the problem and give me the facts; I'll decide.
- Let me know the alternatives, with pros and cons for each.
- Recommend a course of action for my approval.
- Let me know what you intend to do—wait for my approval.
- Let me know what you intend to do—implement.
- Take action. Let me know what you did and how it turned out.
- Take action. Communicate with me only if there's a snafu.
- Take action. No further communication necessary.

We cannot overemphasize here that the key is to *communicate clearly and accurately the nature and scope of your expectations* as you meet with the delegatee. Communicate expectations clearly. Concisely. Precisely. Then release the job and allow employees to handle it—their way. That's right— *their way.* When you delegate, you must be willing to allow mistakes, and you must focus on product, not process.

We urge you to document your delegatory efforts so that you can learn from your mistakes. A notebook devoting a page to each employee works nicely if you use the following format:

EMPLOYEE: _____				
Date	Job Delegated	Level of Delegation Used	Comments	Results

After practicing this technique a few months, you'll no longer say, "If you want a job done right, do it yourself." We predict you'll say, "If you want a job done right, delegate it to the person best able to handle it."

66. Use the Ten-Minute Jump-Start Technique

Are you a procrastinator? If so, you aren't alone. Everyone procrastinates in some area of his or her life. Yes—everyone! Wait a minute—that puts you in some very good company. The key is not to eliminate procrastination—that's setting yourself up for failure. Rather, the key is to manage it. Recognize it when it comes. Do something to move beyond it. Take a bite out of procrastination and get the jump-start you need.

It's very simple. Set a timer, watch alarm, or clock for ten minutes. Then select a project you have shelved through procrastination. Take some action toward moving this project closer to completion. However, give yourself permission to stop working on the project when the alarm sounds. At least 90 percent of the time you won't want to stop because you will have become involved in the project. You see, the problem with procrastinators is not doing the project—it's getting started!

A word to the wise: You must be honest with yourself. If you really want to stop when the alarm goes off, do it! A bit more satisfied. Guilt-free. And productive. Otherwise you won't reap the full benefits of this strategy. Procrastinators of the world—*unite*! Put off tomorrow and do it today. Use this Ten-Minute Jump-Start Technique to successfully move beyond procrastination into productivity.

67. Turnabout's fair play

Emergencies and unpredictable eventualities seem to charac-
terize every manager's workday. They show their ugly face at
one time or another. These unexpected *spoilers* arise because of
changes in priorities, environmental changes, hidden inefficiencies that develop into snafus, sudden user demands, human
error, poor planning (yes, that's right—poor planning), acts of
God, and scores of other unforeseeable forces at work to *make
your day.* The principal measure of the emergency is its uncom-
promising demands on your time and the extent to which it
diverts or derails you from discharging routine duties, capitaliz-
ing on opportunities for innovating, or planning and forecasting.

Most managers have told us the most unwanted time robbers
that invariably interfere with the effective use of their time are
attendance at meetings, incoming telephone calls, visits by colleagues and social callers, unplanned travel, employees with
problems, and visits or calls from customers. (We'll have to
comment here via a sobering observation—we fail to see how a
customer can ever be an interruption.) After all, you're
overhead—customers are profit. We won't let you forget it!

Emergencies themselves can be managed. (Read that last
sentence again.) The difficulty is predicting just which emergency will appear and when. The question, then, that begs to be
asked is—how can a dedicated and resourceful manager, such as
yourself, allow in advance for the time and effort it takes to
manage the unforeseen and unpredictable? That's the purpose
of this developmental activity. Some working estimate of emergency time is needed. Your autonomy to act (not react) can be
explicitly stated and time allocations for taking care of emergency business allocated.

We have found after close analysis of the time consumed by
each of these time robbers that many of them can be pro-
grammed into your workday. For example, knowing how much
time you spend on the phone, in conferences and meetings, with
customers, psychoanalyzing employee problems, and so on, per-
mits your use of time devoted to these interrupters to be pre-
dictable—and therefore manageable. The exact time of an

incoming phone call is almost impossible to predict. (It doesn't take a consultant to tell you that.) However, the prediction of how many phone calls (or visits, or meetings) you will receive and the total amount of time consumed by these distractions is quantifiable.

With this information in mind we suggest you combine two time management options: Take immediate and calculated steps to reduce or manage each time robber. (Sound okay so far?) Then use this more creative approach: Reclassify these emergencies as *unpredictable responsibilities* or *spontaneous assignments.* Going one step further, if these spontaneous assignments were written as performance goals and objectives, they would no longer need to be referred to as emergencies. We're not playing semantics with you. Many activities affectionately referred to as emergencies or unforeseen events are products of poor planning or constitute an escape from responsibility or accountability.

Each of these perceived emergencies can be planned with considerable precision and rationality if deliberate efforts are made to legitimize the time consumed by them. Create an unpredictable-responsibilities or spontaneous-assignments logbook. Divide the log into sections, categorizing each section according to the type of emergency. Then track each emergency with regard to date and time the event occurred, amount of time devoted to the emergency, type of emergency, and so forth. Do this religiously for one month. Live with them. Analyze the results. Catalog them. Evaluate them. Chart or graph them. Then write a performance goal outlining your unpredictable responsibilities. Set attainable and realistic performance standards. Here are several examples, right off the top of our collective heads:

1. Investigate all customer complaints, lodged personally or in writing, and resolve amicably within seventy-two hours. (Disgruntled customers, we might add, communicate their displeasure to at least ten other people.)
2. Using a layperson's counseling and coaching expertise, assist employees in resolving personal problems as thoughtfully and expeditiously as possible.
3. Using established telephone professionalism guidelines, handle all telephone calls within the prescribed limits.

There are, of course, risks of nature and risks of mismanagement. This developmental prescription recognizes that you cannot control acts of God. Legitimate emergencies will occur. However, it will help you begin to program, predict, and manage unpredictable, sometimes chaotic, responsibilities—and sanction their existence in your day-to-day affairs. When you're knee-deep in alligators, it's difficult to remember that your objective was to drain the swamp. (It doesn't take a consultant to remind you of that, either.) However, alligators have swum around swamps for hundreds of millions of years. They've always lived in swamps. If they have a choice, they'd like to stay in swamps. Understanding the nature of swamps and alligators, you might have foreseen that you would meet a few. The failure to drain the swamp isn't the alligator's responsibility. The alligator is just doing what he does best—being an alligator. You probably can't drain the swamp. You're already knee-deep in managerial responsibilities. If you stand there long enough, one will swim up to you. You expect it. You don't know when. But you expect it. When it comes, label it as an "unpredictable responsibility" and deal with it, expertly and professionally.

68. Don't confuse activity with accomplishment

So often when managers have a full plate of endless projects and responsibilities, their ability to effectively manage multiple priorities is tested. The purpose of this developmental activity is to outline two exceptional prioritization schemes. You'll want to pull out your Management by Objectives folder or other performance management index that outlines your strategic and tactical performance goals. Use the Bantamweight or Heavyweight weighting scheme (Exhibit 16) to evaluate each of your performance goals. Once you have assigned a weighted value to each goal, turn to the Activity versus Accomplishment Decision Matrix (Exhibit 17). Follow the procedures outlined for completing the decision matrix.

This sobering development activity will help you see at a glance whether you're confusing activity with accomplishment. You'll discover how well you've stayed on track. Use these prioritization schemes as periodic *barometers* to assess the relationship between what you're really doing and what you've promised to do via your performance objectives. The linkage should be tight. Every task, each project, every assigned role and responsibility should relate directly to your strategic objectives. If you discover that a particular project doesn't fit or falls out of alignment, ask yourself why you're devoting time and resources to a project that has nothing to do with helping you achieve agreed-upon objectives.

Examine each maverick project. Evaluate every nonproductive task. Chip away at or eliminate extraneous or irrelevant pieces of jobs. Slash impertinent responsibilities that have been mindlessly performed because they have always been mindlessly discharged.

69. Use the worry jar

Are you a worrier? Do you paint vivid pictures of future events, creating the worst possible endings? Do you sweat and tremble just thinking about an upcoming presentation or meeting? Do you waste enormous energy reserves conjuring up problems with no solutions?

Worry is the most destructive and least useful emotion we have—and it can sabotage the effectiveness of a manager faster than anything we've seen. The Worry Jar is a simple technique designed to help you refocus that energy, and take control over the situation.

First, get a large jar (or can)—preferably opaque, so that you can't see through it. Cut or punch a hole in the lid. This is your

Worry Jar. (Feel free to get creative and decorate the jar appropriately.)

Next select a DWT (Designated Worry Time). This should be a specific time, once a week (for example, Friday at 4:00). Through the week, whenever you find yourself worrying about something—anything—stop! Grap a piece of paper, commit your worry to writing, fold it, and drop it in your Worry Jar. Tell yourself: "I'll worry about this during my DWT." The subtle psychology behind this technique is taking worry out of your mind, where *it's* in control, and putting it on paper, where *you* control it.

During the week, your Worry Jar will accumulate many worries. At your DWT, open the jar and read your entries. Some of the situations you worried about are history by now and you don't need to worry about them (for instance, Tuesday's presentation—it's over, my performance appraisal—it's done, and so forth). Gloat over the fact that you didn't waste energy worrying about these items; then discard them or burn them in effigy.

Some items will still be pending issues, so now's the time to worry. Focus some good quality time to really worry about these concerns. (Guess what? It's really tough to worry "on cue"!) Once you've worried sufficiently about each of the items, fold them up and redeposit them in the jar, so it will be there again next week.

This technique is great for a whole staff to do together. There's nothing funnier than to see a whole group sitting around a table, vying for the "Most Worried Look." Pretty soon you'll discover the truth of this quote: "Why worry? Either you *can't* do anything about it, so why waste useless energy—or—you *can* do something about it, so stop worrying and do it! Just do it!

Customer Responsiveness

anaging the customer's experience at all points in the cycle of service is absolutely critical to business success. Transforming customer contact people into highly responsive customer advocates who take pride in serving their customers heroically is one of your fundamental responsibilities. Building legendary service is a high calling, one that is based on a bone-deep conviction that there is no substitute for an honest, unshakable belief that the services you provide and the products you sell are the best available anywhere. Read that last sentence again. Its message is central to this series of prescriptions.

Consistent and *sustained* customer-driven performance is possible when the thousands of impressionable moments in which customers come into contact with your organization are managed effectively. Honorably. Genuinely. Uncommon customer courtesy and product quality will help guarantee customer loyalty and repeat business. It'll lead to memorable service. Legendary responsiveness. Distinction.

The prescriptions outlined in the Customer Responsiveness series provide practical strategies to help you build a highly responsive service system. You'll appreciate the distinction between internal and external customers. If enthusiastically and diligently applied, these learning laboratories will help you score high on customer report cards. You'll stand taller. You'll walk with a little more spring in your step. And you'll reap well-deserved dividends in terms of profitability and customer loyalty.

70. A dose of reality brings customer satisfaction

One hour each week, be courageous enough to listen to incoming calls on the toll-free 800 customer call-in number. That's all that's required—just listen and take notes. Take plenty of notes. Vigorously record your insights, regarding perceived product quality; service distinction or pathologies; pricing; customer expectations; complaint resolutions; botched transactions, orders, and reorders; customer satisfaction; and so forth. Ask yourself the following questions: Would I want to continue doing business with us? Why? How have we served our customers heroically? In what ways are we distinctively customer-driven? How can we enhance our service image? What type and quality of service support system do we provide customer contact employees? How customer-focused and service-preoccupied are we? Are we really selling customers what they want? How obsessive is our commitment to managing the customer's experience at all points in the cycle of service? How customer-friendly are we? To what extent is our organizational maze detrimental to customer satisfaction and loyalty? How can we design management systems more conducive to our service strategy? Add a couple of questions of your own. Eye opening, isn't it?

Isn't listening a fine piece of communication technology? As you have no doubt realized, we're fans of it. Prudent and consistent use of listening—just listening to the heartbeat of your customers—will help you score very well on customer report cards. One caution: Please do not limit your actions (remedial or otherwise) only to correcting or applauding the customer-contact people you listen in on (with their happy consent, of course). Until you have answered all of the above questions *and*, through serious introspection, determined your own culpability as one role player in the total cycle of service—until you have done that, until you have examined your own level of responsibility and accountability—please refrain from tut-tutting, finger pointing, or judging anyone else.

Once you've cleaned up your act, act on your cleaning. Once you act, remember—focus on the *behaviors* observed, not the *personalities* involved. Oh, and one more thing—we're absolutely convinced of this: as far as the customer is concerned, there is only the cumulative memory—the obvious patterns, the perceived consistencies or inconsistencies, the gut-level sensitivity of being on the receiving end of care, concern, attention, and responsiveness. Customers—whether your organization's field personnel, headquarters people, the colleague in the cubicle down the hall *or* your suppliers, vendors, and the public—respond favorably to sustained and honest attention.

A must: Add another, phenomenally developmental, dose of reality—answer the 1-800 line yourself. Deal firsthand with customer requests, complaints, and expectations. Spend at least a couple of hours each quarter on the 1-800 line. You'll find yourself *thinking* like the customer. How's that for cultivating a service edge?

71. Is management itself just a service?

Collect market data on two to three best-selling items or product lines without using paper–pencil surveys, compiling thousand bubble-trend analysis charts, or three-hundred-page computer printouts. All that's required is your willingness to travel light, wear a smile that just won't quit, and spend a Saturday in a retail store, surrounded by thousands of potential buyers. Spend one Saturday every other month for six months on the sales floor of one of your major chain customers or executive accounts. Confidently and enthusiastically sell your service or product. That's right, lobby proudly for your company's service or product. Get to know the sales people who sell your products and provide your services, too. They'll be impressed at your commitment to and pride in your service or product.

Imagine seeing the look in the customer's eyes as he or she purchases your product. Feel your own personal satisfaction as a service provider or product champion. Oh, and imagine the look in your eyes as you witness a customer deciding to purchase a competitor's product. "How could they?" you ask. Isn't your product the best on the market?

The issue: How efficient is your service system—you know, the apparatus (physical and procedural) that the service people (internal and external) have at their disposal to meet buyers' expectations? Rationally, of course, we all know that we exist to provide value to the customer. However, there is in most organizations a conspiracy of misplaced priorities and sounds-okay-on-paper mentality that ties people to sterile rules and policies, placing product-driven service strategies first and customer needs second. (We advocate eliminating any rules, policies, or procedures that interfere with customer service.) We believe you'll agree—"rules first, customers second" is not the way to win customers and keep them for life. Examine your service system. What glitches account for much of the tension between office and field personnel? How important are your frontline, customer-contact people? When is the last time you spoke to a flesh-and-blood salesperson? Describe the full cycle of service—from the beginning to end? If each point along the cycle of service is a leverage point, how leveraged is your organization? This next question borders on heresy in the minds of traditional product-driven authoritarian managers. Is management itself just a service?

Are your services and products *taking a bath* in the marketplace or are they *bathing* in the lap of a customer-driven, highly distinctive service system that prides itself in serving its customers heroically?

---

72. Opportunity mapping for distinctive service

Find an example of distinctive service—or specify an end product or component—and backtrack to determine the cycle of service (manufacturing-distribution-delivery process) that produced the desired result. Why? Because as the overwhelming demand for services and products increases, your ability to deliver these efficiently, effectively, and reliably is taxed unmercifully. Legendary service must be managed. In order for it to be managed well, it must be understood. And understanding without experience is the booby prize.

The approach we're recommending here is for you to launch

a thorough investigation. Find out what made the service distinctive. Determine how exceptional quality was ensured. Use this opportunity to judge *how* what went well went well. Inventory the trappings of success. Ask key people who were responsible for the successes how they did it. What were the essential ingredients in ensuring its success? What did you do differently this time to gain such distinction? How were you able to maintain an almost obsessive commitment to managing the customer's experience at all points in the cycle of service? How did you handle system screwups? How did you get past the mediocre? Scale highly defended turf boundaries? Motivate marginal performances? Reward the exceptional ones? Cultivate the heroes? Reach consensus on thorny issues? Maximize resources? Gain top management support? Turn frontline people into customer-oriented salespeople? Develop such a well-conceived strategy for service? Achieve zero defects? Turn ordinary people into extraordinary service providers?

Now, without hesitation, sculpt a vision of service (manufacturing, distribution, delivery) success. Outline the essential ingredients in managing people and resources that produced such a distinctive service-minded culture. Focus on what made it work. From our extremely biased point of view, as disciples of leadership development, we believe the valuable contribution offered by this simple prescription is a reconceptualization of quality and service as top management concerns. Management *must* be constantly preoccupied with service distinctiveness and quality assurance.

Enthusiastically present your findings to the next management level. Sell management on the idea. Ask to be assigned the responsibility of personally delivering these *opportunity maps* (via formal briefings) to every department in the organization. Institute opportunity mapping teams throughout the organization.

73. Awaken sleeping beauty

Select one slumbering service or sleepy product (or one in each product or service family). During the next ninety days, meet extensively with end users, members of the distribution channel, vendors, suppliers, roll-up-your-sleeves colleagues, and people from every conceivable layer impacted by the service or product in your organization. Why? Because most organizations suffer from a crushing quality problem and an embarrassing service posture. Every day we hear new, painful evidence of loss of market share to overseas producers. Why? Because we've investigated dozens of quality and service programs closely, hundreds casually. The hard evidence is incontrovertible: No product has a safe quality lead and no service has a distinct advantage—for long.

Devise a low-investment strategy for radical differentiation of at least one service and one product. How else can organizations satisfy minute-by-minute demands of product-hungry consumers? The antidote: Create ever-changing portfolios of highly differentiated, high value-added services or products. Collect reams of data from quality and value indices. Listen faithfully to end users. Let customer perceptions drive the program. Why not invite customers to the differentiation assessment? Embarrassing? No doubt. Gain customer loyalty? Absolutely. Obtain approvals to relaunch the overhauled product or revitalized service within six months. Then resolve never again to walk past poor quality or tolerate marginal service—in any form—without taking dramatic and immediate action. If this activity moves you (and your people) just one step closer to uncompromised quality and unfailing service, it will have served its purpose.

74. Organize a theft ring

First, determine *who* your competitors are. This is no small task. For example, who are the small domestic firms that are thriving on a tiny piece of your action? These well-niched and hungry competitors can make life miserable, can't they? Who are the big domestic rivals feeding in your once well-fenced and protected pasture? How 'bout the foreign competition? Consider the *who* from competitive sources you wouldn't suspect. For example, Sears' competitor is JCPenney. And Kmart. Wal-Mart, too. And, of course, Mervyns and Nordstrom. Don't forget the catalogers Spiegel and Banana Republic. Leaving out TV home shopping outfits like Home Shopping Club would be a mistake. Who are your oddball competitors? Find them. That's the first step.

Analyze them. Study them. What's their market share? Relative revenue and earnings? Share by segment? Generic product comparison? What kind of and how much training do they provide their employees? How well oiled is their service system? How high is the division manager's spending authority? How responsive is their customer complaint system? To what extent are co-workers accountable to customer-contact people? What makes a competitor's service legendary? Their products household names?

The typical rejoinder we hear is: "Okay, Bil and Cher, we get the point. But how do we get this kind of *competitor snapshot* without wiretaps and spies?" Our evangelical response is to *swipe* them. Systematically. Methodically. Legally. And proudly. Here's how: Organize a theft ring (we owe our thanks to Tom Peters, author of *Thriving on Chaos*, for this idea). Competitive analysis is everyone's business. Your objective is to hire service people, MIS people, manufacturing and accounting people, loading dock personnel, and others. Your colleagues are excellent sources of information. Once they're on the take with you, they'll gleefully inundate you with hundreds of scoops of your competitor's whereabouts and goings-on.

At the next trade association chapter meeting, regional and national conventions or chats with friends and neighbors, members of your theft ring can pick up a great deal of information.

Create ready-made channels (formal and informal) for swapping information and directing it to the right ringleader in your organization. For example, one of your field salespeople may be the first to hear that a competitor is moving from a standardized and limited product line to a more customized, all-inclusive approach. He or she will hear it from one of your best end users, another sales rep, a customer, from an internal sales dispatcher who heard it at his or her bank from a friend, or from a braggart who's doing the market analysis in the competitor's own backyard.

Sign 'em up! Reward 'em. Don't be caught holding the empty bag with the fossilized not-invented-here mentality. It's okay to borrow. To imitate. To mimic. To copy. Use a competitor's idea. Modify it. Retrofit it. Hybridize it. Some of the best managers we know are great strategists. Astute note takers. Unhesitating askers. And shameless thieves when it comes to figuring out what the other guy's up to.

There is, we want you to know, a respectable place for the more traditionally recognized competitor analysis. However, the objective of this developmental prescription is this: Unabashedly, and with mountains of forethought, turn everyone in your organization into vacuum cleaners—swiping as many of the cutting-edge ideas from competitors as is legally and ethically possible. One last word about this prescription before we move on: Consider institutionalizing such a program based on legal and ethical swiping. Copy to enhance. Borrow to customize to meet the needs of your organization. Rotate ringleaders each year. Gang up on the competition. Hold annual Swiped-with-Pride contests for the best-swiped idea. Scale the not-invented-here walls of close-mindedness. Unlock the incredible potential of willing and eager colleagues. Get away from fossilized reconnaissance missions. Reconnoiter shamelessly. Swipe proudly.

75. Honor the chain of service

Everybody has a customer. You may or may not work face-to-face or telephone-to-telephone with the end user of your company's service or product, but you do play a critical role in assuring that the end user is satisfied. It is important for each employee to recognize that he or she is a critical link in the chain of customer responsiveness.

We urge you to take a look at who *your* customers really are. Customers come in two flavors: external and internal. External customers (clients, buyers, vendors, distributors, and so on) are the end users of your service or product. Much less recognized and understood are our *internal* customers—co-workers, other departments, support personnel—all of whom must work together behind the scenes to provide quality services and products. While we acknowledge the need to serve our external customers heroically, we sometimes fail to choreograph a user-friendly internal environment. Complete this activity yourself before assigning it to your staff. Then help them clarify the need to serve everyone they work with in a way that reflects service and quality.

The first step is to clearly define the chain of service. Using the Chain of Service (Exhibit 18), fill in specific names for each category (names of companies, vendors, distributors, the public). Determine your location and your department's location in the chain of service so that you can quickly spot your link in the chain. You may find members of your department represented in more than one link. Be as specific as possible. Remember, the external customer is *anyone* outside your company who uses your service or product. The internal customer is anyone *inside* your company who benefits from your service or product.

When you have completed the Chain of Service assessment and have identified the key players, answer the following questions. We recommend that you put your answers in writing—and commit yourself to actions for improvement while using these questions as launch sites:

1. Who are my direct customers? What do they expect from me?
2. How does my job relate to the end user—the external customer? What effect does my work have on the bottom line?
3. What are three specific ways I can dramatically improve the way I serve my customers?
4. What are three specific ways I can clarify my expectations to my suppliers?

RECOMMENDED READING: *How to Win Customers and Keep Them for Life,* by Michael LeBoeuf, and *Service America,* by Karl Albrecht and Ron Zemke.

SECTION SEVEN

Self-Mastery

Professional development cannot limit itself to the acquisition of external organizational skills alone. It must include
the development and maintenance of a full range of internal
self-management skills as well. The extraordinary demands of
today's business world make it mandatory for organizations to
offer programs that develop the whole person. Lasting loyalty,
trust, and commitment are gained through meeting basic human
needs. Organizations who meet those needs will prosper.

Based on the philosophy that whatever you conceive and
believe, you can achieve, the prescriptions in this section will
help motivate you to reach your fullest potential both personally
and professionally. We'll provide the tools you'll need to en-
liven and enrich your life. Serious exploration and patience will
help you walk the professional path with inner peace. You'll
begin to see your greatness, appreciate your uniqueness and
humanity, awaken to the high calling of service to others, and
move toward a more self-fulfilled personhood, characterized by
peace of mind, joy, health, satisfaction, and purposeful living.

76. Let the real manager out

This adventure in leadership exellence is not for the 99-percent
committed manager. You have to own your leadership role a full
100 percent or return the keys to the company car and corporate
jet. One of the most important developmental tools you'll ever
use is what we call an *intensive journal*. Designed to capture
your thoughts and experiences, the intensive journal serves as a
long-term recapture mechanism for sustained development.
The uncanny value such a journal brings to your managerial
growth is its built-in *progressive abstraction* feature. (That is to
say, it enables the well-disciplined manager to progressively
move his or her professional focus toward health and wholeness
at his or her own tempo.) Its therapeutic value is amazing. It
systematically evokes and strengthens one's inner capacities by
evolving from a totally subjective (and therefore subconscious)
vantage point and proceeds without analytic or diagnostic

categories. Since these recorded thoughts and experiences become part of your personal history and are recorded systematically in your own words, you can accumulate tangible and factual validation of your personal and professional growth and transformation *in process*.

The effective psychological principle operative here is that when you are shown how to reconnect yourself with the contents and continuity of your managerial unfoldment, the inner thread of movement through corporate *battlefields* and *playgrounds* reveals itself through your insights and feelings. This self-integrative principle, this professional life review, makes it possible for you to experience (re-experience) times of exaltation and times of despair, moments of hope and anger, crises and crossroads, successes and failures, promotions and commotions, shining moments and dull misses.

You will find that the intensive journal is an unfailing boomerang (written, produced, and directed by you) that provides grist for your professional mill. Many executives ask how long they should continue to make journal entries after they have gained important insights. Our usual response is forty to fifty years, at least. You're worth every bit of the time and energy you devote to you. See Exhibit 19 for an example of an intensive journal format to get you started.

77. Repair rocky roads with forgiveness

This developmental activity is a must: Pick two to three rocky interpersonal relationships (preferably inside, but certainly worth considering outside of work—longtime friends, relatives, co-workers, family, former spouse). Review, in your own mind, the scenario leading up to the split. What factors led to your interpersonal distancing, the process of disengaging, of relationship decay? What is it about the battered relationship that has enough value in it to continue to produce occasional interactions, if any? In what ways do you choose to avoid contact? Describe the reasons behind the deterioration. What's in it for you to continue to value relationship desolation over relationship repair? How do you feel about your ability to manage disagreement or conflict? Study the rift. Analyze it. Place it under your intellectual and emotional *microscope*. Examine every bruise, each angry salvo, every tear, each decision to perpetuate the adversary relationship.

Consider repairing the relationship. Start with forgiveness. What are ten things you can do to move toward a personally satisfying outcome? It may mean you've done all you can. It could mean releasing the past and moving beyond the limitations posed by such a dysfunctional relationship. However, you don't know that yet. So make the first move. Do it! Move toward a more complete personhood.

78. Lights, camera, action!

If you've ever been involved in drama, you know the value of rehearsals. This technique borrows the lessons from the stage and applies them to your skill as a manager. What specific skill areas do you want to develop? Where do you feel particularly vulnerable? Is it conducting a performance appraisal? Discussing a poor work habit? Disciplining a marginally performing employee? Sending your budget request to your manager? Selling an idea to senior management?

Identify the particular issue you want to handle more effectively, and write it down. Next, find a person willing to rehearse successful scenarios with you. Audition for the part. Dramatize the situation. Be emphatic. Have your "co-star" realistically role-play the part of the other person. You, of course, play the self you'd like to be.

This backstage rehearsal offers you the opportunity to test

several options. It allows you to experience handling the simulated situation effectively. If you're going to make mistakes,
make them during this test flight. Do a couple of full-dress
rehearsals. Then move on to your command performance. Take
the new you to the real world. Put on your costume and walk
confidently out onto the corporate stage. Lights, camera, action!
"Opening night" is a piece of cake. All that's left is for you to take
your bows, enjoy the applause, and begin rehearsal for another
part.

79. Travel in your Mobile University

How much time do you spend in your car? On a plane? Do you
find yourself frustrated by the lost hours spent commuting to
appointments? If you feel you're wasting valuable time through
travel, have we got a deal for you! Transform your vehicle into a
Mobile University. Never before has it been easier to learn.
Simply pop a cassette into a recorder, and learn while you earn.

We cannot overemphasize the value of becoming a cassette-
tape junkie. A mountain of research supports the power of
spaced repetition—listening to presentations on a tape cassette
over a period of time. With each session, you'll gain new insights
and strengthen the effects of the information groove in your
subconscious.

Through this wonderful instrument—the cassette recorder—
executive development is just an earful away. Learn valuable
lessons from the pros. Here's how to get the most benefit from
your Mobile University: Determine two or three key issues,
questions, or developmental need areas you have an interest in
pursuing. Then select a tape related to that area. Keeping your
issues in mind, listen to the entire tape. We recommend that you
carry a small recording device in the vehicle with you. As you
get *Aha*'s from listening to information on the tape, record your

insights on the recorder. (Refrain from taking notes while driving. It can be hazardous not only to *your* health, but to that of other motorists.) Listen to each tape several times. Remember the value of spaced repetition. But don't just listen. Always ask yourself: "How can I use this information? What can I do now? How does this apply to me?"

Where do you gain access to these wonderful resource tapes? Fast-forward to the next sentence! Try the library, retail stores, record stores, direct mail, your company's learning library, your professional organization, local colleges and universities. Here are a few more excellent resources:

Tape Rental Library, Inc.
One Cassette Center
Rt. 29
P.O. Box 107
Covesville, VA 22931

National Speakers Association
4747 N. 7th Street, Suite 310
Phoenix, AZ 85014
(602) 265-1001

Nightingale–Conant
7300 N. Lehigh Avenue
Chicago, IL 60648
1 (800) 572-2770

Masters of Success
The Allan–Michaels Corp.
120036 Acklen Station
Nashville, TN 37212
(615) 791-2880

80. Know thyself

Everyone recognizes the importance of skill development and many will even support the idea that companies should pay for it. But we feel a need to raise a very critical question: How can you initiate a targeted development program if you haven't identified areas of improvement? This includes self-improvement! Before you can successfully see payoff for investments in self-development, you have to build on existing competencies.

This developmental ramp provides you with a tool to help facilitate this process. It helps you take a valuable look at yourself, in terms of your experience and leadership capabilities.

Use the Professional Skills Inventory: A Self-Assessment

(Exhibit 20) to assess your skills. Let us offer a few "words of wisdom" as you complete the inventory. First, be completely honest. Remember—when you cheat, you're cheating only yourself!

Second, when identifying the skills you are now using or have used, include skills you use off the job as well. Many times you have opportunities to practice leadership skills while participating in community activities, religious functions, or a professional trade organization where your employer doesn't require you to take part. These collateral involvements can transfer directly back to the job.

Third, don't equate "time on the job" with level of proficiency. Some folks have ten years of experience, while others have just one year of experience times ten! When evaluating your performance proficiency, consider "5" to mean you *excel* in this area. (We mean you almost walk on water!) A "1" indicates that your capability is not too strong at all—you really need work in this area.

After you've completed the inventory, identify your top five strengths, and the five skill areas you would most like to develop. Then schedule a meeting with your manager, share your insights, and, in conjunction with your manager, target specific areas of improvement.

By the way, if you're feeling really brave, we recommend that you give a blank inventory to your manager. Request him or her to evaluate you, based on his or her perception. This is a sobering experience.

81. Ask twenty-one gut-wrenching questions

Spend some contemplative time answering each of these questions. If answered honestly and thoughtfully, each question will have a deepening effect upon you. Each is an odyssey in itself, taking you one step closer to leadership excellence.

- How often and in what ways do you give balanced, believable, and timely feedback about the specifics of day-to-day job performance so that people are clear on where they stand and how they're doing?
- When is the last time you sat eyeball to eyeball with a subordinate and discussed what he or she learned as a result of the training just attended?
- What specifically is the difference between acceptable, unacceptable, and exceptional job performance?
- When was the last time you modified or eliminated a demeaning rule or regulation in favor of co-workers' self-esteem or self-respect?
- When, and under what circumstances, do you encourage people to become too dependent on you?
- In what ways do you use your position to control rather than to guide and support people's contributions?
- What is it that prompts you to tell people what they want to hear instead of leveling with them?
- When was the last time you felt threatened by an individual's exceptional skill, ability, or physical attractiveness?
- With what types of people do you work the best?
- How important would it be to take five minutes up front at the next scheduled training session and encourage the group's commitment and participation?
- When was the last time you were *stuck*, unsure about how to proceed, and hesitated to ask anyone for advice?
- What is the single most important value in your life? What sacrifices would you be willing to make to protect that value?
- When was the last time you completely *relaxed* and enjoyed yourself? What were the benefits?
- What is the worst experience you ever had to endure? What powerful growth lessons did you learn from that experience?
- If you could trade places with anyone for one day, who would it be? What do you think your day would be like? How would you view relationships, money, success?
- If you were able to give a speech thanking everyone who

helped you achieve success, which individuals would you include? Why? Write the speech you'd like to give.

- If you knew that your safety could be *guaranteed,* what one adventure risk would you like to experience?
- If a genie offered to grant you three wishes, what would they be?
- Select three self-defeating *habits* you'd like to eliminate and transform each of them into a *preference* for something else. What would those preferences be? Why?
- Write your epitaph and funeral service sermon. How has this writing experience enriched you?
- What has been your greatest failure as a child? As a young adult? As a parent? As a spouse? As a manager? As a human *be-ing.* What can you, or have you, learned from it?

This process will awaken an inner energy, a self-actualizing pulse, which will guide you into new awarenesses and personal dimensions. As you explore your own *inner space,* expect new potentials and transpersonal vistas to surface. It's not often you're required to descend into the bowels of your consciousness through such introspection.

We have found this self-evaluative process to be stimulating and transforming as layer upon layer of the *real you* unfolds. The psychological literature is filled with instances that show how any shift or change in your outer awareness is always preceded by a shift in inner awareness.

Spend no less than an hour on each question. Accept no less than your best thinking. Devote quality time to this activity. See this as a marvelous opportunity to evaluate your motives, perceptions, assumptions, and biases. In fact, when we decided to include this activity in your developmental package, we reasoned that you owed it to yourself to be perfectly candid with the only person in the world that knows the real you—*you!*

82. Sell-yourself-on-yourself commercials

Do you talk to yourself? Do you talk out loud? Now for the tough question: Do you answer? (We believe those who do are the truly sane people—they definitely know a good conversationalist when they find one.) Seriously, research says we *all* talk to ourselves—and 75 to 95 percent of what we say is usually negative. Inventory your negative "self-talk." "Boy, was I stupid, What a klutz! If I had half a brain!" It's time to reprogram your messages. What you tell yourself has a direct relationship to your ability to handle stress, deal with people, and achieve your goals in life. We unabashedly advocate sell-yourself-on-yourself commercials. Here's how: Develop a set of short, positive statements about yourself. We call them Personal Empowerment Triggers (PET phrases):

- I am cool, calm, and collected in all situations.
- I have all the energy I need—and some to spare!
- I sizzle with zeal and enthusiasm to do all I need to do.
- I speak before groups with ease and confidence.
- I practice total quality management.

Create PETs to reflect areas you want to develop. A few rules are in order as you prepare your list:

1. *Keep your PETs positive.* Instead of saying "I am no longer tired," say, "I am filled with energy."
2. *Keep your PETs in the present tense.* Avoid phrases like, "I'm going to be able to speak in public with confidence someday." Use positive launches like, "I speak before groups with ease and confidence; I am a consummate speaker."
3. *Use the KISS (Keep It Short and Simple) technique.* Don't confuse the issue with a long, involved statement filled with qualifiers and descriptions. Simply state what you'll do in as few words as possible.
4. *Develop two types of PETs.* One set includes a core curriculum: PETs that are related to your general attitude

and well-being. (I am rich, well, and happy in all areas of my life.) The other type relates to specific development goals you are currently focusing on (for example, I handle discipline problems among my employees effectively and in a timely manner; I complete my monthly reports on time).

Now, how did it feel to write your PETs? Be honest! Most managers admit that after the initial awkwardness of saying positive things about *themselves* disappears, this activity feels pretty good. But the best is yet to come. Record your statements on a cassette tape. Be as upbeat and enthusiastic as possible. Then, on your way to and from work, pop the cassette into your tape recorder. Listen as your own voice reinforces your success with your personalized sell-yourself-on-yourself commercial.

What? You're having difficulty coming up with PETs? Not to worry! Lots of folks have difficulty with positive programming. Our prescription: Use "Glamor Grammar." Simply run through the alphabet and identify positive words beginning with each letter. Then preface each word with an "I am" (for instance, I am attractive, I am brilliant, I am creative, I am daring, I am enthusiastic). Be a legend in your own mind. Personal Empowerment Triggers are morale boosters. We've seen managers literally transform depression into a positive, creative mood simply by using this strategy. Don't feel frustrated if you don't believe yourself initially. For example, you'll say, "I am able to delegate with ease and confidence. . . . Right. What a joke!" This self-criticism is quite natural. You have accumulated a lifetime of negative self-talk. Naturally the subconscious is going to rebel against anything positive initially. But it's just a matter of time. You have to fake it till you make it! Keep programming your expected improvement with the PETs. You'll see a definite shift in your attitude, capabilities, and actions.

83. Straight from the horse's mouth

Do you have your eye on a certain career position, but have no idea how to prepare for it? If it's located in another department or responsibility area, it becomes doubly difficult, since your manager may have limited information about it. But don't despair. This technique will get your developmental ball rolling.

Create a list of key questions you have about the position. You might want to include these just to get you started:

- What are the key responsibilities of the job?
- What training would be helpful in preparing for the job?
- What competencies are necessary?
- Whom does this person interact with, and how?
- What is the toughest challenge associated with the position?
- What is the best advice for someone interested in the job?

Share your list of questions with your manager. Ask for feedback in terms of additional issues to include. Then, schedule an Information Interview with the person currently holding that position. Send that person an advance list of questions so that he or she will be prepared. Take your cassette recorder (so that you don't waste time taking notes). Listen attentively as the incumbent tells you everything you wanted to know about the position. Then compare the requirements and needs for the position with your current capabilities and experience. Develop a plan of action to prepare yourself to assume higher responsibilities. Align your current education, knowledge, and experience with what is needed to succeed in the prospective assignment. Make the necessary course corrections.

We must emphasize that it takes time to prepare for the next step in your career. When the position becomes available, it's too late to start preparing. Forewarned is forearmed, so begin now, even though someone else is firmly entrenched in the position.

84. Life is only a dream

The thought of including an activity on dream interpretation was both appealing and frightening for us. Frightening because of the high probability that most managers will make superficial attempts at understanding and interpreting these nocturnal videos—despite the facts that sleep occupies a third of our lives and that more than one-fourth of all discoveries come from dreams. Appealing because dreams, second only to psychoanalytic understanding, are the royal road to self-discovery and transformation. Having so justified this activity, we invite you to explore the world of dreams as a leadership development mechanism.

Dreams are nocturnal messages from ourselves to ourselves. Some are prophetic; others call for emotional and physical growth and transformation. Still others are warnings to clean up our human acts. Many are reenactments of events from the previous day's activities. Dreams are truly our magic mirrors toward self-discovery and empowerment. The power of dreams to lift the dreamer to heights of unprecedented personal or professional success is well documented.

We agree with Swiss psychologist Carl Jung, who said:

> People will do anything, no matter how absurd, in order to avoid facing their own souls. They will practice Indian yoga and all its exercises, observe a strict regimen of diet, learn theosophy by heart, or mechanically repeat mystic texts from the literature of the . . . world—all because they cannot get on with themselves and have not the slightest faith that anything useful could ever come out of their own souls.
>
> Jung, C., *The Undiscovered Self*, (translated by R. F. C. Hull), Boston: Atlantic Monthly Press, 1957.

Every dreamer has the potential to become an inventor; an innovator; an entrepreneur; an exceptional manager; a writer; a composer; a better professional; a happier, healthier, and wealthier human being. An experience from a single dream can shape our destiny and bring many rewarding ideas and insights. Solutions to life's worrysome problems. Comfort. Healing. Discovery. Recovery.

Keep a dream log for no less than six months. If you do not intend to devote that kind of time to this important project, we suggest you turn to the next page in your professional development. When you're ready, revisit this prescription—and discover who you really are. We've included Thirteen Dream Appreciation Hints (Exhibit 21) and Fourteen Basic Dream Recall Hints (Exhibit 22) to get you started. However, we decided not to include more information on dreams for the purposes of this manual, since even a brief (and just) treatment would take volumes. We elected instead to provide you with a bibliography (Exhibit 23) of several outstanding resources that are filled with research-based helps and techniques. One of the guiding principles we used was to rein in the flights of speculation and fantasy and to insist that hypotheses be supported by as much clinical evidence and scientific rigor as possible. We also encourage you to speak with a psychologist or other certified dream interpretation (appreciation) professional before stepping out too deeply into the *nocturnal video store* owned and operated by you.

We'll conclude with a few thought-provoking messages about dreams:

> Again, no one is sure, apart from faith, whether he is awake or asleep, seeing that during sleep we believe that we are awake as firmly as we do when we are awake. We believe we see spaces, figures, movements; we experience the passage of time, we measure it; and in fact we behave just as we do when we are awake. We spend half our life asleep, in which condition, as we ourselves admit, we have no idea of truth, whatever we imagine, since all our perceptions are illusory. Who knows, therefore, whether the other half of life, in which we believe ourselves awake, is not another dream, slightly different from the first from which we awake when we suppose ourselves asleep?
>
> If we dreamt in company and the dreams, as often happens, chanced to agree, and if we spent our waking hours in solitude, who doubts that in such a case we should believe matters reversed? Finally, as we often dream that we are dreaming, and thus add one dream to another, life itself is only a dream upon which other dreams are grafted and from which we awake at death, a dream during which we have a few principles of truth and goodness as during natural sleep. These different thoughts which dis-

turb us are mere illusions, like the flight of time and the empty fancies of our dreams.

Pascal, Blaise, Pensées, pgs. 936 and 937.

No single theory can do justice to the richness of dreams, and one very simple fact about them—which almost all psychotherapists neglect completely— is their direct relation to the event and thoughts of the previous day.

Faraday, Ann, Dream Power, New York: Berkley Books, 1972.

There would not be a dream from the unconscious except as the person is confronting some issue in his (her) conscious life—some conflict, anxiety, bafflement, fork in the road, puzzle or situation of compelling curiosity. This is, the incentive for dreaming— what cues off my particular dream on a particular night—is my need to "make something of the world I am living in at the moment."

May, Rolo, The Courage to Create, New York: Bantam Books, 1975.

85. Zen and the art of managerial maintenance

A manual on executive development wouldn't be complete if it failed to include an activity on meditation. As practitioners, we unabashedly recommend it. Meditation is one of the most powerful tools available for integrating body, mind, and spirit— for centering on all levels of being. It has been practiced since the beginning of time, and methods for quieting the mind are found in every culture, East and West.

    The spectrum of the meditational experience has absolutely no parameters, no clear-cut boundaries. Feelings range from the blissful to the powerful, visions from all-encompassing to unfathomable darkness, and sounds from endless chatter to a single resonating note. The self-actualizing gifts you will receive are priceless and enduring. You'll receive a deepening—a transpersonal sense of who and what you are. An increased connection with the universe. A peace and serenity that will sustain you through corporate storms and organizational earthquakes.

Meditation is an excellent way to position yourself to hear the still small voice. Gain access to inner guidance. Crystallize a grander and more complete vision, based on wisdom and inner knowing. It is a technique of letting go, of recovering the wiser you, of accessing grander dimensions of being. It's the art of managerial maintenance.

Historically, meditation is a practice aimed at religious experience. It differs from prayer because prayer is predominantly a verbal turning to an external deity. Meditation, on the other hand, is not concerned so much with directing petitions to an external God, but with inducing changes at a deep level within the meditator. Although verbal means are used (chants, seed syllables such as "OM"), generally the emphasis is on introspective nonverbal practices. Some of the most common meditational practices are "stilling the mind" by excluding thoughts and images, concentrating on one's breathing, watching the flame of a candle, or mentally sustaining such images as a mandala, light, the face of a figure or guru, a lotus, and so forth.

Whatever the system, effective meditation creates radical changes in a meditator's way of experiencing the world. The meditative state has been classified as an altered state of consciousness; however, it closely resembles the peak experience level of functioning described by Abraham Maslow in *The Farther Reaches of Human Nature*. A central theme throughout all meditational disciplines seems to be a felt connection with a spiritual reality beyond (yet inclusive of) the self. Such self-actualization and personality changes lift an individual's awareness to a level that is expressed as self-transcendence, unity, oneness with all, *samadhi*. Respectable data from hemispheric research suggest that the cortical hemispheres are affected similarly by meditation, and inhibitory and excitatory influences within each hemisphere may be generated and evolve as disciplined meditators progress. This whole brain, transcendent consciousness consists of letting go of all limiting identifications, whether earthly or heavenly, in order to reach that exalted supreme consciousness that is unfettered with the bondages of human weakness.

The goal of all meditation systems, whatever their ideological orientation or source, seems to be to transform the ordinary consciousness experienced during the waking state (via a particular meditative discipline), transcend egoistic selfishness, and rebirth to a new level of wider-awake functioning.

A great number of scholarly works and empirically sound experiments have helped to improve our understanding of the essentials, benefits, and implications of the meditative process. Substantial foundations have been made in determining the basic types, functions, and affects of meditation. Sufficient ground has been covered for us to include a brief description of several noteworthy research findings over the last fifteen to twenty years.

Some of the results based on the data generated throughout two decades of research reflect clear-cut statistical inferences, while other data are more general in nature. Although these results are in certain cases very simple, they are intended to remedy basic misunderstandings about the meditative process itself and to serve as some of the raw material for this somewhat advanced technique for managerial growth:

1. It was probably inevitable that meditation would be described as a relaxation technique. Studies have found that meditation causes significant decreases in oxygen consumption, carbon dioxide elimination, respiration rate, cardiac output, and heart rate; increases in skin resistance; increases in the intensity of slow alpha waves; and conscious relaxation.

2. The general picture that is emerging suggests that meditation may enhance psychological well-being and perceptual sensitivity, reduce anxiety, reduce alcohol consumption, rehabilitate myocardial infarctions, and effectually treat bronchial asthma and insomnia.

3. Although profound relaxation is reported, meditative relaxation is perceived as only one among many spontaneous and often dramatic changes in perception and experience.

4. It takes a fairly mature level of personality development just to practice meditation, especially forms of meditation based on observing the moment-to-moment mind-body

processes, fears, anxieties, humiliations, rages, depression, despair, self-doubt and even ecstasies that self-discovery entails. Clinically, meditation strengthens the ego rather than transcends it. On the other hand, all psychological growth occurs when the individual is able to renounce outworn, infantile ties to things and give up or modify behaviors that have become restrictive, maladaptive, or outgrown.

5. Meditators as a group are more psychologically and autonomically stable, less anxious, more self-actualizing, and appear to be more inner-directed.

6. Marked decreases in sleeping and eating occur during long-term meditational practice. Often meditators report a sense of physical lightness, greater energy levels, and greater well-being during periods of intense meditation.

7. Exceptionally vivid dreams are common during meditational practice.

8. Meditators tend to be more present-focused rather than dwell on the past or future. In addition, meditators are more positive in their outlook and enjoy increased spontaneity.

9. Studies of brain physiology during meditational practice have used the EEG (electroencephalograph) to measure brain wave activity. Preliminary tests show that meditators may have enhanced ability in right hemisphere skills and greater flexibility in shifting from one hemisphere to the other in response to specific right-left brain tasks.

Meditators who persist in meditational practice over time, particularly transcendental meditation, appear to have successful outcomes in terms of overall health and well-being. These changes include self-perceived increase in the capacity for intimate contact, increased spontaneity, positive self-regard, and inner directedness.

As you face the challenges ahead, consider adopting meditation and adding it to your managerial curriculum. We have touched only the tip of the meditational iceberg. We hope we've given you enough incentive to begin your meditational practice. We have found that when you meditate on a regular basis, a new, more expanded you emerges. We encourage you to allow that submerged essence of your wiser self to bubble up into every-day life so that its power and serenity permeate every activity and each relationship.

You have an opportunity to explore and discover deeper parts of yourself. To transform yourself. To know yourself. To help get you started, we have included a brief meditation entitled Pendulum of Light. You'll find it in Exhibit 24. There are a number of excellent meditation resources available. You may want to begin by contacting professional organizations and societies for more information. Most cities have wellness centers and holistic health centers, which offer classes in a variety of meditational disciplines. You may also want to consult bookstores and libraries for literature on the various meditational techniques and health benefits of sustained meditational practice.

86. Snapshot solutions

How many times have you gone to bed and, as you struggled to go to sleep, all the problems of the day paraded through your mind? And with each problem, you received flashes of insight on how you should have handled them! Well, stop "shoulding" on yourself and snap out of it. This developmental activity will help prepare you to handle those problems more effectively.

Purchase a photo album—the kind that has a column of overlapping pockets. Purchase a set of insert pages—this snapshot album will be a growing resource for you. Each page represents a typical problem area with which you must deal. It can be as specific as necessary. For example, one manager was having difficulty responding to excuses his employees used to explain why their projects were incomplete. So he used a separate page for each excuse he'd heard.

Another manager wanted to improve her ability to deal with a marginally performing employee, so she selected a separate page to represent each work habit (for example, tardiness, excessive use of telephone for personal calls, sloppy work area).

A sales representative was uncomfortable handling objections and used a separate page to list each objection and its Rx.

Soberly and honestly identify your problem areas and list them on cards (cut and sized to fit the clear plastic pocket in the album). Slip each into the top pocket of an album page. Now, brainstorm a variety of options to handle each problem area. List each option on a separate card. We recommend that you take advantage of other managers' experiences and ideas and ask them to participate in your brainstorming session. Host a brainstorming party and ask each colleague to BYOI (bring your own ideas).

Once the solution options are printed on cards, slide them into the pockets layered under each problem area. The next time you're confronted with a challenge in one of your identified problem areas, simply turn to that page in your solution book, flip through the pockets, and choose the snapshot solution that seems best for the specific situation you find yourself in.

87. Rendezvous with your past

With sober and serious introspection, write your autobiography. Interview relatives, friends, high school teachers, college professors. Revisit old neighborhoods, if possible. Connect yourself with the past. Spend a nostalgic afternoon browsing through old photograph albums. Take a trip to the attic, dust off the old trunk and reminisce. Collide head-on with your past. Descend into the depths of your childhood and youth. Excavate your toddler shoes or baby blanket or first finger painting. Resurrect childhood memories. Revisit old yearbooks. Unpack that old high school or college sports sweater. Admire memorabilia. Reflect. Reminisce. Recollect. Remember. Resurrect. Then, write.

We suggest that the length of the autobiography should be

not less than one typewritten page for each year of your age. If you are forty-one years old, your autobiography should contain at least forty-one pages; if you're fifty-five, fifty-five pages of text. Spend quality time on this project. Your personal evolution and unfoldment have brought you to where you are today. Each day is the launch site for tomorrow. Your well-researched life review will be a springboard for the new you.

Our hope is that you will proceed faithfully from the first page to the last. That you will emerge not only with a substantial understanding and appreciation of where you've been, but also with a revitalized psyche and renewed interest in introspection, self-evaluation, and self-definition. Because you are a constellation of experience. You are an evolving personality. A micro-universe unfolding. A human being who must successfully matriculate through this multicurriculumed classroom we call life.

No doubt this will be an exacting task. For self-exploration is as much self-recovery as it is self-discovery. The review process is a sobering one. It calls for a serious attempt to make one's individuation process conscious. Sustained investigation and serious reflection are necessary prerequisites for just the right amount of psychic material to percolate up into your conscious awareness. The difference between your natural unfoldment, which runs its course unconsciously, and the one that is consciously realized, is tremendous. The therapeutic effects are lasting. The self-integration transforming. So go ahead. Do it now. Rendezvous with your past and take a backward glance.

88. Stay street-smart

Take a focused sabbatical. These are paid work-related development assignments. Sanctioned. No-nonsense. Well-timed and well-supported growth experiences. The length of your sabbatical is, of course, between you and your manager and your organization. It depends on a number of things, mainly the nature of the sabbatical, replacement availability, current and projected work assignments, receptivity of top management, and so on. In our estimation, focused sabbaticals should be designed solely as short-term learning laboratories. Their intent: Sharpen, fine-tune, and develop new managerial skills. Put new life into high-potential (and bored) managerial bones. A well-timed sabbatical can be a breath of fresh air. Get operationally involved full time in some facet of organizational life. Get involved in some sort of start-up operation somewhere in the company. Go off-site to troubleshoot problems. If you're in headquarters, plan a field tour of duty. If in the field, accept a headquarters assignment. Become a loaned executive. Spend six months as an adjunct trainer in management development. Assist in a site relocation or a plant opening or closing. Research, design, and implement a companywide management development program. (It'll take at least a year to put this together.) Is cross-functional job rotation out of the question? How about a speaking assignment that requires you to be the company's spokesperson for an important environmental or social issue? Why not establish an Office of Creativity and Innovation? (Now that's a good idea. One worth pursuing—really!)

Agree on the learning outcomes up front. Midcourse revisions are fine. Touch base frequently. Apply yourself. Above all—enjoy yourself! Immensely.

89. Use sabbaticals as learning laboratories

Take a company-sponsored educational leave of absence. These sabbaticals are offered solely to provide higher education opportunities for high-potential, thoroughly committed, completely loyal, nonexpendable executives and managers. Appropriate

learning laboratories would include university and college summer programs, overseas study, special skills certifications from
recognized institutes of advanced learning, university degree
programs, and various licensing programs (a pilot's license
would be nice). The purpose here is to add formal credentials to
an already star performer. Go ahead, get started. Why wait?
Work out the details, and go for it—now!

90. Become the little professor

Have you ever heard the axiom "Those who know, do; those
who don't know, teach"? As professionals in the field of human
resource development, we cringe at the idea of seeing unqual-
ified people educating others. But as with most humorous quips,
we must admit there is a grain of truth in this one. Never are we
more susceptible to learning than when we are put in the position of having to teach.

This prescription asks you to determine a specific area you
need to develop. The topics are limitless; for example, you may
want to improve your skills for time management, empowering
people, technical writing, financial management, conflict resolution, or feedback. Once you have selected the topic, design
and develop a three-hour training program on it. Consult with
adult educators and curriculum designers. Upgrade, revitalize,
and modify in-house course materials on the subject.

After you have developed the content and materials, find an
audience. Potential platforms include your company, local community colleges, the Chamber of Commerce, professional societies, and so forth. Include a detailed postworkshop critique, so
that you can refine and enhance your program. Developing a
quality learning experience is one of the toughest activities
you'll do. You'll need to decide what is important. Relevant.
Absolutely necessary for performance improvement. Work

closely with training and development specialists. Put on your training hat. Become the little professor for a day.

We predict that you will astonish yourself with how much *you* learn by teaching others.

91. Multiple listings for personal growth

Professionally we use lists as a time-management tool. Memory-jogging mechanisms. Procedures outline. As an organizer or detail *marquis*. A to-do list. However these lists are employed, their purpose seems to be to present information clearly, concisely, and orderly. The *multiple listings* we propose will help you organize your thoughts around important themes. Uncover proclivities toward health, wealth, and wellness. Crystallize core values and beliefs. Lasso long-forgotten experiences. Spawn life-enriching insights. Identify self-actualizing tendencies. Magnify attitudes and assumptions. Unzip memories. Immortalize successes and italicize failures. Revisit old patterns. And focus on defining the real you. The updated you.

The self-definitional lists (Exhibit 25) are designed to help you integrate your beliefs, attitudes, and experiences. You'll be asked to get beneath the surface on key life issues. To get past the obvious. You'll need a notebook, pen or pencil, and courage. Select one of the lists as a starting point. Each week for the next fifty-two weeks, generate 101 items for the particular list you've chosen for that week. Write the list in one or two sittings during one day. The sheer volume of entries will dredge up life-changing information from your subconscious mind. Be sure to complete each list. After you've completed the list, review it with an eye toward themes. Use whatever taxonomy you want to classify the entries into categories or themes.

Ask yourself penetrating questions, such as these: What have I learned from this list that will help me become a better leader?

A more mature person? Enrich my thinking? Create positive changes in my life? Identify my strengths? Expose my weaknesses? What would the top ten priorities be for each list? How can I learn from mistakes? In what ways can I celebrate my successes? What personal and professional goals *will* I establish *immediately* to improve myself based on what I have *discovered* from the entries on each list?

Internalize what you've learned. Choose to be deepened by this provocative and highly introspective experience. Move toward a fuller and richer personhood.

92. Targeted professional growth areas

Many of life's biggest problems can be solved by taking incremental steps toward their improvement. This strategy is amazing in terms of its simplicity and overwhelming results. Begin by making a list of thirty-one areas of your professional development you want to monitor and improve. These are your *delectables!* Then create a file for each delectable. That makes thirty-one files. Everyone's list will differ, but here are a few delectables to get you started:

1. Conducting Performance Appraisals
2. Managing Clutter
3. Correspondence
4. Running Meetings
5. Managing Stress
6. Communicating with My Manager
7. Motivating Employees
8. Meeting Deadlines
9. Ongoing Projects
10. Budget
11. Balancing Work and Personal Time
12. Handling Interruptions
13. Giving Constructive Criticism
14. Customer Service Awareness
15. Staying Up-to-Date in Current Profession
16. Frustrations

17. Dealing with Conflict
18. Fears
19. Procrastination
20. Positive Attitude
21. Cold Calls
22. Computer Skills
23. Staff Meetings
24. Delegation
25. Interaction with Marketing Department
26. Successes
27. Employee Relationships
28. Journal Writing
29. Presentation Skills
30. Planning
31. Personal Review

Now, the fun (and growth) begins. Every day examine the topic that corresponds to the calendar date. For example, if today is the 23d, find file number 23. That becomes your Selectable Delectable for the day. Spend fifteen to thirty minutes focusing on that specific topic. Capture your thoughts on paper. Add magazine articles to your file. Course information. Breakthroughs and highlights. File any information that relates to each selectable delectable behind the appropriate number.

What makes this technique so powerful? We're glad you asked. Each month, as you repeat the process, you will accumulate a running commentary of your progress in thirty-one areas of your professional development! You'll begin to spot patterns, identify common threads, and chart monumental successes. Here are some specific examples from a computer manager's entries:

April 2—Managing Clutter: My desk is a disaster! The in-box is overflowing. Bob asked for the customer feedback report, and it took me a half hour to locate it! *Action:* Clean off top of desk. Empty in-basket.

May 2—Managing Clutter: Cleaned off my desk, and have kept it organized for two weeks. Hooray for me! It feels great. Now—focus on files. Boy, are they a mess—stuffed full and hard to find information. *Action:* Clean top file drawer.

April 13—Constructive Criticism: I met with Roger to discuss his personal use of telephone—I felt awkward talking with him and was intimidated when he challenged me.

Also spoke with Amy about her marginal performance. Felt it went much better this time. *Action:* Practice! Anticipate reactions. Be prepared. Keep track of their progress.

May 13—Constructive Criticism: Met with Roger again. This time I had my act together and was able to be firm and clarify my expectations. We agreed on actions and have put them in writing. Much better! I'm meeting with Jack tomorrow to discuss absenteeism and feel good about my preparation. Amy's performance is much improved—I told her so.

Notice how you can review the prior month's entries before recording current entries. This gives you a running commentary of progress. Use action items to trigger steps for improvement. You'll find tremendous satisfaction in reviewing your progress in so many areas of your professional life. So dig in and build your Selectable Delectables file for success!

Targeted Innovation

The best-performing companies realize that one of the keys to sustained technological health and human resource excellence is cultivating an innovation-rich work environment. Long-term profitability and economic stability demand meeting the rapidity of change and relentless competition with systematic and well-trimmed innovation. More and more, progressive, tuned-in managers realize that idea power is an essential ingredient in ensuring their competitive edge.

Innovations, whether in products, market strategies, technological processes, or work practices, give organizations a distinct advantage over competitors who smother the creative impulse and drown the entrepreneurial spirit. The prescriptions outlined in this section are designed to help you learn how to manage innovation, think creatively, solve problems creatively, and see creativity as a manageable resource. We encourage you to use this intuitive technology. Apply it strategically. Use it to complement more traditional problem-solving methods. To revitalize existing decision-making schemes. To faithfully embrace it as a necessary element in achieving organizational objectives. To use it as a *technology ramp* that will produce innovative solutions to nagging business problems.

The fundamental message for these prescriptions is that creative breakthroughs are lucrative, repeatable, and reliable economic events that can be expertly managed and reasonably predicted. Creativity is a learned skill. We repeat—creativity is a learned skill. In today's economy, managers will either innovate or stagnate. We hope you'll choose to tap the creative genius within yourself, your people, and your customers. You'll find this to be an invigorating chapter in your managerial development.

93. Compose a laundry list for fast-paced innovation

Using the Breakthrough Management® lists outlined in the Laundry List creative problem-solving technique (Exhibit 26), privately or as a group member, generate as many ideas or associations as you can to solve an existing problem. Put on your thinking cap. We're talking about using your imagination and intuition here. Why? If responding to the tremendous challenges and accelerated change in the marketplace with almost unbelievable alacrity to internal and external customer whims is your superordinate goal, fast-paced innovation will be your chief enabling mechanism.

The guiding premise here is this: Be willing to innovate—or stagnate. Be willing to personally symbolize innovativeness in your daily affairs. Clear your calendar one afternoon this week and use the Laundry List to start the ideation process. Wrestle with a thorny issue. Shoot a sacred cow. Tackle a systems snafu. Unplug a communication bottleneck. Clear away a hurdle in a market strategy. Reconceive the middle manager's role. (Oops, have we gone too far? We think not!) Redesign an automation scheme. Realign. Elasticize. Dynamite. Uproot. Tighten. Refurbish. Immunize. Tantalize. Dismantle. Reverse. Magnify. Decentralize. Economize.

94. Expose yourself to virgin territory

Organize a small task force composed of five to seven people who are unfamiliar with or have limited experience with a new product line, plant start-up, customer contact program, proposed policy change, and so on. The problem could be how to institute a fair and equitable employee benefits or compensation package, reduce the costs of operating D-line by 15 percent, ensure zero defects in XYZ assembly, institutionalize innovation, increase first-time complaints resolutions by 10 percent, or modify existing information retrieval systems to make them more user-friendly.

Lead the group in generating ideas to solve one of these problems. That's right! We're asking you to lead a group of people who are totally unknowledgeable about the subject area.

Before you throw your martyred hands up in despair, consider this—a half-dozen or so highly reputable studies of the process of invention reveal the following fact: The lion's share of invention comes from the wrong person in the wrong field in the wrong industry with the wrong credentials and the wrong connections at the wrong time with the wrong user. (You may want to read that again. We'll wait.)

Typical among the invented-by-impostor scenarios are Kodachrome, invented by two musicians; synthetic detergents, by dye-making chemists; a birth-control device, by a gynecologist *and* dentist, of all people; the ohm measurement in electricity, by a mere Jesuit math teacher. Camouflage patterns used in the military came from the cubist art of Picasso and Braque, the unbreakable U. S. military code used during WWII was based on the Navajo language, and (our favorite) manned flight was invented by two bicyclists—the Wright brothers.

Extend the idea. Talk to lead users. Ask them to help design a more customer-friendly service system. If you're a manufacturing manager, ask a distribution manager to suggest ways you could improve your operations. If you're in distribution, ask sales; in personnel, ask new hires. If you're the chief operating officer (COO) or CEO, ask the custodian, quality assurance manager, maintenance supervisor, secretary, or office services manager. Cross the border. Trespass. Use *outsiders* as your passport to fast-paced innovation.

95. Use the "Evolving Showcase" to get ideas

Institutionalize innovation. Get everyone involved. Use the Evolving Showcase (Exhibit 27) to solicit ideas from a wide variety of people. Convert one of the meeting rooms into an idea gallery. Post an organizational problem, one that would attract the most interest, on flip chart paper. The idea is to allow employees to browse through masterpieces (ideas from colleagues) that have been recorded on chart paper posted on walls. Permitted to come and go as they please, employees are to add new ideas, jot down questions, record insights, restate the problem, and so on. Depending on the scope and criticality of the problem, the Evolving Showcase could remain open for several days or as long as a week. Take action on the ideas. Use sessions like these as *innovation ramps*. Involve people.

We believe it is vital for senior managers—in all businesses, in enterprises of all sizes and dimensions—to champion the innovative spirit, to move beyond the traditional problem-solving schemes, to give people in various functions (management information services, manufacturing, accounting, internal sales, maintenance, personnel) ample opportunities to innovate. Our bet is, you'll be glad you did.

96. Management development 101

This will not be easy! It requires considerable thought and focus—and energy. Develop a list of 101 ways to serve customers heroically. Add to that a list of 101 ways to motivate people. Supplement those lists with 101 traits of an effective leader. You're not through yet. Top it off with a list of 101 mistakes you've learned from while working with people. Quite frankly (you do want us to be frank, don't you?), you'll probably want to stop before you get to the magic 101 figures. And, yes, to answer your question—101 *is* an arbitrary figure. We're hoping, though, that you'll see the value in stretching the limits of your imagination; going beyond the obvious; exploring the nooks and crannies of service distinctiveness; energizing people and assessing human error.

Most leadership development programs fail to address the soft-skill areas. We think they've missed the point—they've eaten the menu instead of the meal. We stand proudly on our soapbox and argue that there are measurable, quantifiable predictors of leadership success and failure—outside the traditionally sterile *basics* like performance appraisal, disciplinary procedure, organization communications, delegation, managing multiple priorities, and budget. These more ephemeral and harder-to-quantify predictors are vision, energy, passion, love for ambiguity and paradox, imagination, unconditional positive regard, empathy, consistent persistence, unfailing grace under fire, incredible patience, purposeful impatience, intense devotion, uncompromised integrity, and unconquerable resolve to produce the best product and deliver heroic service. This is the stuff exceptional leaders are made of. These are the qualities and attributes you'll uncover at the high end of each of your lists, after you've run out of the traditional fix-its and do-its taught mindlessly in most management development programs.

After your lists are complete—enthusiastically and passionately, with every cylinder in your managerial engine humming—apply what you've learned. Become a human achievement accelerator. Now reward yourself. Think of 101 ways to celebrate success for less than $101!

97. Kindergarten 102

This prescription will bring back memories—and allow you to let the child out! It will stimulate creativity, help manage stress, and open your mind to options. It does require one small investment: Buy a container of Play-Doh. Yes, that's right! Play-Doh! For a few dollars you can pick up several colors, and really have fun! It'll be putty in your hands.

Find a space of uninterrupted time and create a sculpture. Take time to enjoy experiencing the Play-Doh. Squeeze it, roll it, smell it! Get totally wrapped up in it. Concentration itself is an excellent aid in inducing complete relaxation. Relaxed and centered managers are much more capable of dealing effectively with people, projects, and marketplace paranoia.

But this is only the beginning. As you create your Play-Doh masterpiece, be aware of the thoughts and ideas running through your mind. We recommend you have notepad and pencil nearby. It is not uncommon for lucrative ideas and solutions to materialize during this creation phase.

After you've created your masterpiece, examine it. Compare your sculpture to your leadership style. For example, one of our clients created a car. Not just *any* car, but a Jaguar—red, of course! His analogy was that he expects the best, and that's what he's always looking for. So—the "best" drives right up and honks its horn. He won't settle for anything less.

Another manager created a pancake and analogized that a pancake must be cooked on both sides to be good—no one wants a half-baked pancake. Yet, she felt she sometimes failed to commit totally to a project and gave only lip service—hence, half-baked support. The pancake was a reminder to her to be *totally* commited.

Let your imagination soar as you develop your analogies. Then keep your Play-Doh masterpiece on your desk or bookcase as a constant reminder of the management philosophy or style you want to master.

98. Use home movies to imagine solutions

Creative visualization is a mental imagery technique, which uses your imagination to create physiological and psychological realities. A compelling amount of research confirms that visualization can play a significant role as a transformative and restorative tool. Its therapeutic effects and healing power are extraordinary—and well documented. To quiet an unbelieving mind, we have provided a laundry list (Exhibit 28) of a few recent, scholarly investigative efforts on the subject of mental imagery and visualization. Western science is rediscovering the incredible transforming powers of visualization. Accept it as fact. Believe it. Don't miss out on this exquisite piece of mental technology. You will need it. The marketplace has become a battlefield. Organizations can be torpedoed. Careers can go up in smoke. Whole markets can disintegrate. You'll need balance. Inner peace. Harmony. You'll need visualization.

The purpose of this developmental activity is to help familiarize you with the basics of creative visualization and provide a safe place for you to enjoy your home movies. You'll find that you are the screenwriter, producer, director, star, camera person, and choreographer of your home movies. You can carry your set with you anywhere you go. You can unreel any scenario or drama you want to view. You can even pick up where you left off without detracting from the message contained in your miniproduction. Conscientious practice will help enhance your imaginative abilities and allow you immediate access to your previously untapped subconscious (and superconscious) abilities. You'll be able to tap into your creativity. Expanded sensitivity and awareness of the world around you are also by-products of applied visualization.

The premise of this activity is that your thoughts create your reality. Trust that statement. We're serious. We mean it! Conscientious and sustained practice moves possibilities closer to probabilities and transforms probabilities into realities. We've witnessed the powerful effects of visualization hundreds, thousands of times. Your movies began the day you were born. You add footage every fleeting moment of every day, through every conscious and subconscious thought and act. Generally speaking, most of our everyday thinking is composed of a circular series of nothing more than a trivial pursuit of gnawing (and boring), insignificant details of our lives. Not only is this kind of mental chitchatting unproductive, it prevents us from creating. Discovering. Growing. Potentializing.

Visualization can help you eliminate the noise, the incessant droning of mediocrity, the obnoxious chatter of the insignificant. For a minute or so, close your eyes and clear your busy mind of all thoughts. If any thoughts wander into your consciousness, just acknowledge them and let them pass through. The objective is to stop *thinking* for just one minute. Sixty seconds.

How did you do? Wasn't easy, was it? Unless you are a seasoned meditator (or went to sleep), you undoubtedly found it almost impossible to completely stop the flow of your thoughts. You're not alone. You're in good company. If you witnessed a stream of thought trivia parade by, be reassured that even the most brilliant and creative among us are often preoccupied with thought fragments that clutter our thinking and trash our reverie.

Most of our thinking is like a leaky faucet, constantly dripping thoughts and wasting valuable insights. One of the keys to both creativity and true relaxation is freeing our minds of nonproductive thoughts and conserving the mental energy it takes to launch more worthwhile thoughts. Before you read any further, let's prove how much of an *imagineer* you are. Look at the nearest lamp, picture, office equipment, or momento. Notice its shape, its texture, its size. What color is it? Is it wood, metal, or glass? Examine it closely. Observe how the light casts shadows. Touch it. Does it feel soft or hard, cool or warm, smooth or sharp? Totally absorb yourself with the object you have selected. Walk around it. Observe it from all directions. Pick it up. Is there anything about it you haven't noticed before? Is it heavy or light in weight? Now put it back where you got it and return to your seat. Take one last look at it.

When you are satisfied that your examination has been complete, close your eyes and picture in your mind's eye the object you've gotten to know. Spend the next two or three minutes re-creating the object by forming a mental picture. How was that for a home movie? Did you surprise yourself? What you've just experienced is mental imagery.

What people see on their "mental screens" varies from person to person. Some see images in technicolor, others see black-and-white pictures. Some see clearly defined and detailed images. For others the images are fuzzy or shadowed. Still others simply "sense" that the essence of the object is there but somehow can't seem to "see" it. Whatever your experience, whether you "saw" it or "sensed" it, you created some sort of mental image.

The following brief encounter with a guided visualization will be transformative. Enriching. Revitalizing. Have someone who is sensitive and conscientious about providing you unconditional and loyal support read the visualization slowly and with conviction. You may even want to record it yourself on an audio-cassette tape. A copy of the script is provided below.:

Adjourn to a quiet, secluded, relaxing place. Sit comfortably, plac-ing your hands in your lap or at your side. Take one of those smooth, relaxing breaths that start deep in your abdomen and are drawn up past your stomach and finally into your lungs. Inhale slowly through your nose. Exhale by blowing the air slowly and purposefully through your parted lips.

And again—inhale—exhale.

Once more—inhale slowly—exhale through your parted lips.

Reposition yourself if you feel tense. Move your shoulders. Roll your neck. And once more, take a deep relaxing breath—slowly exhale.

Imagine, in your mind's eye, that you are on an exquisitely beautiful island in the South Pacific. You find yourself standing on a deserted beach where the sand is warm and white and clean—you feel relaxed and at peace—

The sound of the gentle breaking surf is soothing. You move close enough to dip your toe into the warm ocean water. The whole atmosphere is one of peace and serenity. You come upon a cove and decide to spend time there. Exploring—resting— The soft ocean breeze caresses your body and blows back your hair as you walk into the soft breeze.

Now listen carefully to the easy rhythm of the small waves.

You have found a calm and beautiful and private place. The silence is broken only by the sound of the surf embracing the beach, the sea gulls searching for lunch, your clothes dancing in the gentle breeze.

You are safe here. It is a place of peace and healing. Stop walking now, and kneel down. Touch the warm sand. Pick up a handful and watch as it falls through your fingers. Now lie down in the sand and enjoy the quietness and solitude of this mo-ment.

Notice the softness and warmth of the sand that is dry and molded around you. Be aware of the warmth of the air and the consistency of the sand pressing against you . . . from the heels of your feet that press into the powdery softness of the sand to the back of your head as it, too, rests in the sand . . . . Become serious and introspective for a moment.

Is there some problem you are facing in your life or career that concerns you—that you would like to eliminate?

Feelings of anger over a broken promise?
Anxiety over a missed opportunity?
Fear of the unknown?
An emotion that is destructive?
A physical illness?

Or, perhaps confusion about your value—or anxiety over the contributions you want to make—or resentment toward a colleague or customer?

Using the first image that comes to mind, simply give the thing you want to be rid of some physical shape.

It could be round like a ball, rectangular like a file cabinet, linear like a rule.

Now, can you see the shape of this thing? Keeping your eyes closed, slowly sit up and see yourself relaxed and comfortable. Envision this thing clearly. Feel its weight, its texture, its size. What color is it? Is it warm? Cold? Rigid? Flexible?

Place all of your concentration on this object until you know every line, every contour, every inch of its form, every detail. Visualize it so clearly in your mind that you sense every part of it. Now imagine that it is small enough to fit into the palm of your hand.

Notice that if it is in your hand, it is no longer in your body—it is no longer a part of you—you won't find it at work—because it's here! The thing you want to be rid of is in the palm of your hand. You are much bigger than it. You now control it. You have power over it. You have reduced it. Miniaturized it. Nullified it.

When you are ready, slowly extend your arm and place this thing about a foot away from you on the sand. Now look at the thing you want to rid yourself of as it sits on the sand.

Rise, now, to your knees and begin digging a hole in the sand. As you dig, you realize that you have dug a hole considerably larger than the object itself. Notice how powerless the object is.

Continue digging the hole until you feel a sense of completion, a belief that you've dug the hole as big and deep as it needs to be.

When you are ready, take the object in both of your hands and drop it or push it, or toss it forcefully into the deep hole. You have dug the hole so deep that the object is hidden in the darkness at the bottom of the hole.

Using both of your hands begin to push sand into the hole. Use your arms to scoop sand around and into the hole. Continue filling the large hole until the hole is completely covered with sand. Now flatten the surface area of the sand. Smooth it so evenly that the traces of your fingertips disappear.

Stand now and move a few steps away from the entombed object. The thing you would be rid of is beneath the sand. What are your thoughts now as you put this thing—this barrier, this negative force in your life—behind you?

Become aware of how you feel at this moment—

Now, slowly and confidently move farther away from the burial place. Turn your back on it. You feel empowered. Deepened somehow. More confident. Self-assured.

Look now and see how close the tide has moved. It reaches your feet and cascades over your toes. The water is just right—so warm and refreshing—

Enjoy your victory. Believe in your power to eliminate obstacles. To extinguish the fires of doubt. Welcome your newfound freedom. Believe in yourself.

Feel the warm ocean water cover your ankles. And once again, hear the ocean sounds—the white breakers moving to shore, the laughter of the sea gulls.

Move out farther into the water now—feel the cool ocean spray. You feel like a child again. You may walk or run, or play still farther out in the surf, if you enjoy the feeling and still feel comfortable.

Or you can simply return to the shore and relax, allowing the sun to dry your body. Simply choose where you want to be and delight in the feeling—

When you feel safe and secure and refreshed, just know that the thing that blocked your good is buried deeply in the sand and is covered with water. And that each wave's pilgrimage to shore buries it deeper and deeper.

Now—when you are ready—come back to the sound of this room. Breathe slowly once again. And smile. You've just experienced a deepening. A transformative mental trip. A more enriched personhood.

Thank you for taking the time to enrich yourself. Heal yourself. Move yourself toward wholeness. Use this beautiful visualization again. Often. It'll add life to your years and joy to your life.

99. Climb the staircase to brainstorm ideas

This technique has been used for hundreds of years and is one of the basic ideational processes used in the Breakthrough Management® process. The key to effective free association is to generate one idea and use that idea to generate another idea, which is then used to generate a third idea, and so on until a useful idea is found. The process takes the problem solver progressively away from the original word by focusing on each word that is presented.

For example, the problem of how to develop a product name for a new cereal or breakfast food could involve selecting a key symbol that relates directly to the problem. In this case the symbol or word could be the word "taste." The first impression that the word "taste" calls to mind might be "bite." Our spontaneous reaction to the word "bite" might be "crunchy." Next we might intuit the word "nuts." This last set of associations might lead to the new product name: "Almond Crunch" or "Bite O' Nuts."

Perhaps another example will help. Suppose the problem was how to effectively discipline a marginal employee. As a result of using the Staircase prescription, a group generated the following abstractions: appraising, performance, command, military, regimented, unyielding, steel, strong, muscle, exercise, health, mature, and ready. Using the list of thirteen progressive impressions generated to help solve the sample discipline problem, the team brainstormed ideas for each one (according to step five in the process below). For example, associations for the word "appraising" included objectivity, judge, and written; "military"—force, target, and chain of command; "unyielding"—unforgiving, unchanging, and rigid; "muscle"—massive, bully, and overpower; "ready"—now, set, equipped.

After these associations were made, the group developed ideas for each of the progressively abstracted words, making a list of all possible connections. Here are some of the insights derived: A marginally performing employee will not have a "long life" here. We need people who are "ready" and willing to do the work. When job "performance" falls to the marginal level, we've got to "exercise" our right to bring the poor performer back to "health." We'll have to put some "muscle" into our "appraisal." We're responsible for the marginal performance if we continue to allow it to go unchecked. Until the performance is acceptable, we'll have to be more "regimented"—or even more "militaristic" and "unyielding" in our expectations. Our resolve must be as "strong" as "steel" to help offset the employee's weaknesses and move him or her toward more acceptable performance.

The solution: Bring the employee back to "healthy," productive "performance" now through "targeted" training to offset weaknesses. Then apply managerial "muscle" if the employee is "unyielding" or refuses to take responsibility for meeting acceptable performance standards.

The advantage of this approach is that it increases the likelihood of generating relevant and practical ideas that relate in some way to the problem. The level of abstraction from the initial word or concept chosen depends on the number of free associations generated. The number of generations that produces the most substantive associations seems to occur after ten to fifteen connections have been made.

The steps for this progressive abstraction technique are to:

1. Jot down a word, concept, or object that relates directly to the problem statement, in whole or in part.
2. Free-associate from the first word or concept that comes to mind.
3. Record that idea and free-associate from the first word or concept that comes to mind relating to the word. Withhold all judgment as to its relevance to the problem.
4. Continue to free-associate with each word-to-word connection until a list of seven to ten associations has been developed.
5. Starting with the first word at the top of the list, brainstorm all possible associations with that word. Develop ideas for each of the words that appear on the initial list until all possible connections are made.

6. Review the list of associations (usually from one hundred to two hundred) and select those that have special application to the problem.

Jot down a few challenges of your own. Use this technique to generate some unique (and workable) solutions. It'll require about an hour of your time. Mentally jog up and down the staircase a few times. After you're familiar (and comfortable) with the technique, deputize trusted colleagues to serve as your think tank and tackle a mutually pressing work issue. You'll be pleasantly surprised at the results.

100. Use constellations of experience to see associations

Suppose you are meeting with a few colleagues in the conference room. Your absorbing discussion is interrupted by the sound of plastic ricocheting off metal, followed by a human cry. As you glance in the direction of the commotion you see that someone has just tripped over a chair. The person picks up the chair, looks at the group sheepishly, apologizes for the ruckus, and politely leaves. What's your immediate impression of this person? Klutz? Bungler? Clumsy oaf? Incompetent clown?

Okay, five minutes later, someone else walks into the conference room, and she, too, falls over the chair. Ten minutes later, another person stumbles over the same chair. The whole scenario occurs again when someone else enters. What's your opinion now? Probably that the chair is in the wrong place. Congratulations, you've just recognized an emerging pattern. A tendency. Or trend. You might even be so bold as to generalize this trend into a rule that says anyone entering the conference room through the east door will trip over the chair—assuming, of course, the chair is left there.

The human mind is very good at recognizing patterns, trends, sequences, and the like. Patterns help us understand the world we live in. We generalize repetitions into rules. Possibilities become probabilities. Probabilities may become everyday occurrences. Everyday occurrences become norms. Norms become a way of life. Most norms are productive; however, some generally accepted behaviors, processes, procedures, or attitudes can have detrimental effects if allowed to remain. The purpose of this prescription is to help you identify patterns and tendencies associated with your work environment. Once recognized, these trends can be evaluated for their merit or debilitating influence. Those that lead to a healthy corporate environment should be kept. Nurtured. Spawned. Those that smother the quality of work life or stifle quality and productivity must be modified. Realigned. Eliminated.

We've identified ten constellations of experience to get you launched (Exhibit 29). Collect ten sheets of paper. Entitle each with one of the patterns or trends outlined in Exhibit 29. Starting with the first trend, Cycles, think of as many Cycles as you can that relate to work and people. Then move to Distributions. Brainstorm examples of as many types of Distributions as you can, related to work, productivity, people, customers, and so forth. Movements is next. Then go to Probabilities, and so on until you have spent quality time on each. After you've immersed yourself in this task, ask colleagues to join you in identifying entrenched or emerging patterns or trends.

Evaluate the results. Keep what works. Publicize it. Garnish it. Water it wherever you find it. Immortalize it. Take immediate steps to eliminate constellations of negative experience. Neutralize debilitating experience. Uproot any act or condition that compromises your organization's ability to carry out its mission.

101. Go with the ideational flow

A couple of our favorite ideation exercises serve as the chief components in this creativity-inducer prescription. This activity will test your resourcefulness and ideational fluency. It'll encourage you to think beyond the commonplace, the traditional, the habitual. When applied to everyday managerial problems, these two gems of ideational cunning will help you to see challenges from new and more exalted points of view. With practice, you'll operate from grander perspectives. You'll become much more adept at seeing the big picture. You'll think more strategically. Your ideational connectivity will expand. Original and novel thoughts will even emerge. (That prospect may be a little frightening to some people.) The demands of today's marketplace, however, require leaders who are visionary. Who are comfortable seeing grander gestalts and exploring blurred corporate landscapes. Who are quixotic (inventive) in their thinking. Globalized thinkers. Who believe in progress. Thrill at a creative insight. Who are awestruck at novelty. Appreciate intuition's lightning-fast kiss? Who always operate two or three chess moves ahead of sluggish competitors who smother the creative impulse.

Exercise 1—Select seven items generally found in a wastebasket or garbage can. Then generate ten uses for each item. Think as fast as you can. Avoid judging your ideas, no matter how unusual or bizarre they seem. Do not concern yourself with practicality. Just generate uses for each of the seven items as rapidly as possible. We have included examples of several items found in garbage cans and their uses in Exhibit 30. If you're having difficulty generating ideas, consult our sample list to help propel your creativity. Otherwise, complete your own list and then compare it to the sample. This activity tests your ideational fluency—how good you are at generating a large quantity of ideas in a short period of time. The next activity will test your resourcefulness and ability to see beyond the obvious. It's called "what-iffing" and requires you to break the rules. To climb out of mental ruts. To gain fresh insights.

Exercise 2—Ask yourself what-if questions. For example:

- What-if the human life expectancy were two hundred years?
- What-if the workweek were only three days long?
- What-if everyone could slam dunk a basketball?
- What-if each country were responsible for manufacturing and distributing only one product?

- What-if the only source of long-distance transportation were a helicopter?

Some possible answers for the question "What-if the human life expectancy were two hundred years?" could be

- Retirement age would be extended to, say, age 150.
- We'd have to buy more birthday gifts.
- We could put off things longer.
- The gift for our centennial wedding anniversary would be a tour of Fort Knox.
- Disability insurance carriers would go broke.
- Your midlife crisis wouldn't begin until age one hundred.
- You'd still have a full set of teeth and a full head of hair at age one hundred.
- Families would tend to be larger.
- We'd go through puberty at age sixty.
- Waiting lines for movies and sports events would be "peopled" by personal brokers to prevent the moviegoer from standing in line.

Now apply each of these techniques to the real-world work environment. Generate as many uses as you can for a suggestion box, Rolodex, office of innovation, derailed project, empty file cabinet, stack of personnel manuals, 1-800 number, spare conference room, old computer printouts, masking tape, and so on.

What-if you could read a customer's mind? What-if customer contact people were the highest-paid employees? What-if all employees must approve every policy change? What-if there were no limit to salary increases? What-if there were no educational or experiential requirements for job qualification? What-if every computer broke down? What-if there were a four-day workweek? What-if there were no managers or supervisors?

The EXHIBITS*

EXHIBIT 1.

Vehicle Parts Sheet (13)

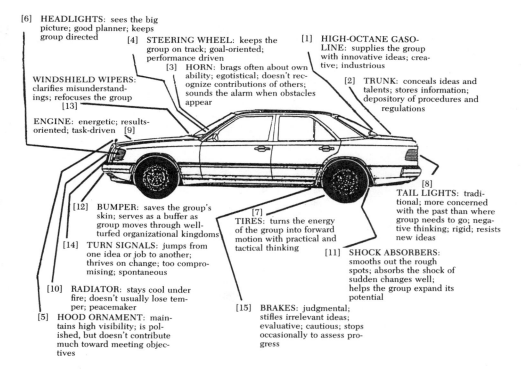

[6] HEADLIGHTS: sees the big picture; good planner; keeps group directed

[4] STEERING WHEEL: keeps the group on track; goal-oriented; performance driven

[3] HORN: brags often about own ability; egotistical; doesn't recognize contributions of others; sounds the alarm when obstacles appear

[1] HIGH-OCTANE GASOLINE: supplies the group with innovative ideas; creative; industrious

[2] TRUNK: conceals ideas and talents; stores information; depository of procedures and regulations

WINDSHIELD WIPERS: clarifies misunderstandings; refocuses the group [13]

ENGINE: energetic; results-oriented; task-driven [9]

[12] BUMPER: saves the group's skin; serves as a buffer as group moves through well-turfed organizational kingdoms

[14] TURN SIGNALS: jumps from one idea or job to another; thrives on change; too compromising; spontaneous

[10] RADIATOR: stays cool under fire; doesn't usually lose temper; peacemaker

[5] HOOD ORNAMENT: maintains high visibility; is polished, but doesn't contribute much toward meeting objectives

[7] TIRES: turns the energy of the group into forward motion with practical and tactical thinking

[8] TAIL LIGHTS: traditional; more concerned with the past than where group needs to go; negative thinking; rigid; resists new ideas

[11] SHOCK ABSORBERS: smooths out the rough spots; absorbs the shock of sudden changes well; helps the group expand its potential

[15] BRAKES: judgmental; stifles irrelevant ideas; evaluative; cautious; stops occasionally to assess progress

(Adapted from Alfred A. Wells, "The Car." In *1982 Annual for Facilitators, Trainers, and Consultants.* San Diego: University Associates.)

EXHIBIT 2.

Vehicle Inspection Work Sheet (13)

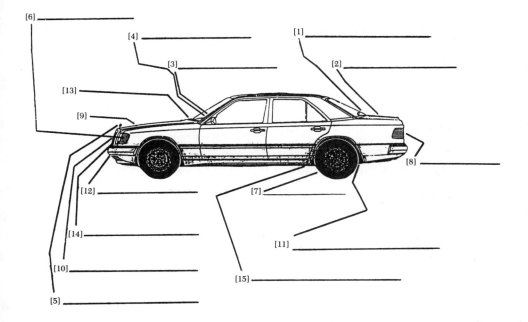

EXHIBIT 3.
Parts Is Parts Summary (13)

Car Part	Group Member	Number of Times Selected
1. High-Octane Gasoline		
2. Trunk		
3. Horn		
4. Steering Wheel		
5. Hood Ornament		
6. Headlights		
7. Tires		
8. Tail Lights		
9. Engine		
10. Radiator		
11. Shock Absorbers		
12. Bumper		
13. Windshield Wipers		
14. Turn Signals		
15. Brakes		

EXHIBIT 4.

Checkup from the Neck Up Questionnaire (23)

	Low				High

1. How satisfied are you with how your team handled this activity?   1 2 3 4 5

2. How clear was the team about its goals and tasks?   1 2 3 4 5

3. How well did team members listen?   1 2 3 4 5

4. To what extent did *you* contribute to the work of the team?   1 2 3 4 5

5. To what extent were *all* team members involved in this activity?   1 2 3 4 5

6. To what extent were you bothered by overparticipation by one or more members?   1 2 3 4 5

7. To what extent were decisions made by consensus?   1 2 3 4 5

8. How well did the team organize itself for its work?   1 2 3 4 5

9. To what extent did the team recognize and define its problems, resolve conflicts, and deal openly with interpersonal issues?   1 2 3 4 5

10. What was the level of enthusiasm and commitment to this activity?   1 2 3 4 5

Our team's biggest strengths:

Suggestions I have to improve the team's effectiveness:

EXHIBIT 5.
"Two-by-Two" Profile (24)

Develop a "working definition" for each word or phrase, and select the
one that best describes your preference. Then, using the same definitions, select the word or phrase in each pairing that best describes the
values of your work environment—what is rewarded?

Participation / Individuality
Risk Taking / Follow the Sure Path
Recognition / Results
Cooperation / Competition
Ethics / The End Justifies the Means
Structured / Flexible
People-Focus / Task-Focus
Education / Experience
Work Time / Personal Time
Activity / Accomplishment
Formal / Informal
Individual Incentive / Team Rewards
Intuition / Facts
Planning / Doing
Innovation / Standard Operating Procedure
Change / Status Quo
Leading / Following
Open Door Policy / Chain of Command
Productivity / Quality
Short-Term Profit / Long-Term Profitability

EXHIBIT 6.

Influence Profile (32)

Listed below are twenty-one pairs of statements that explain how you view your behavior at work. Consider your role, responsibilities, and personality as you assign point values to each pair of statements below. Allocate a total of three points for each set of two statements. Base your point allotments on your judgment of how much each statement applies to your ability to influence others.

For example, if the first statement strongly describes you,

   _3_ A.

   _0_ B.

However, if A and B are both characteristic, but B is a little more characteristic,

   _1_ A.

   _2_ B.

1. ____ A. I can punish or penalize colleagues who do not cooperate with me.
   ____ B. Colleagues know that I have connections with very influential people within our organization.
2. ____ E. My position in our company gives me the authority to direct or delegate work activities.
   ____ F. My colleagues like me and enjoy doing things for me.
3. ____ C. Colleagues respect my work experience, knowledge, and skills.
   ____ D. I either have or can obtain immediate access to information that is important to other employees.
4. ____ G. I can reward and support colleagues who cooperate with me.
   ____ A. I can punish or penalize colleagues who do not cooperate with me.
5. ____ B. Colleagues know that I have connections with very influential people within our organization.

     ____ C. Colleagues respect my work experience, knowledge, and skills.

6. ____ D. I either have or can obtain immediate access to information that is important to other employees.

     ____ E. My position in our company gives me the authority to direct or delegate work activities.

7. ____ F. My colleagues like me and enjoy doing things for me.

     ____ G. I can reward and support colleagues who cooperate with me.

8. ____ A. I can punish or penalize colleagues who do not cooperate with me.

     ____ C. Colleagues respect my work experience, knowledge, and skills.

9. ____ B. Colleagues know that I have connections with very influential people within our organization.

     ____ D. I either have or can obtain immediate access to information that is important to other employees.

10. ____ C. Colleagues respect my work experience, knowledge, and skills.

     ____ E. My position in our company gives me the authority to direct or delegate work activities.

11. ____ D. I either have or can obtain immediate access to information that is important to other employees.

     ____ A. I can punish or penalize colleagues who do not cooperate with me.

12. ____ E. My position in our company gives me the authority to direct or delegate work activities.

     ____ B. Colleagues know that I have connections with very influential people within our organization.

13. ____ F. My colleagues like me and enjoy doing things for me.

     ____ C. Colleagues respect my work experience, knowledge, and skills.

14. ____ G. I can reward and support colleagues who cooperate with me.

     ____ B. Colleagues know that I have connections with very influential people within our organization.

15. ____ A. I can punish or penalize colleagues who do not cooperate with me.

     ____ E. My position in our company gives me the authority to direct or delegate work activities.

16. ____ B. Colleagues know that I have connections with very influential people within our organization.

    ____ F. My colleagues like me and enjoy doing things for me.

17. ____ C. Colleagues respect my work experience, knowledge, and skills.

    ____ G. I can reward and support colleagues who cooperate with me.

18. ____ D. I either have or can obtain immediate access to information that is important to colleagues.

    ____ F. My colleagues like me and enjoy doing things for me.

19. ____ E. My position in our company gives me the authority to direct or delegate work activities.

    ____ G. I can reward and support colleagues who cooperate with me.

20. ____ F. My colleagues like me and enjoy doing things for me.

    ____ A. I can punish or penalize colleagues who do not cooperate with me.

21. ____ G. I can reward and support colleagues who cooperate with me.

    ____ D. I either have or can obtain immediate access to information that is important to colleagues.

(Adapted from J. R. French, Jr., and B. Raven, "The Basis of Social Power." In *Studies in Social Power*, ed. D. Cartwright. Ann Arbor: University of Michigan Press, 1959.)

EXHIBIT 7.

Influence Profile Scoring Sheet (32)

Scoring   Go back through each of the sets in the instrument and add all the scores you gave to each of the A, B, C, D, E, F, and G statements. Start with the A statements and tally those scores; go on to the B statements; then total the C statements, and so on, until you have recorded a score in each of the Statement Totals below. (To check your addition, your total score for all sets should equal 63.)

Statement Totals   <u> A </u> + <u> B </u> + <u> C </u> + <u> D </u> + <u> E </u> + <u> F </u> + <u> G </u> = 63

Your Influence Matrix

A	Tyrannical				
B	Networking/Alliance				
C	All-Knowing Guru				
D	Informational				
E	Pecking Order				
F	Charismatic				
G	Midas				

0 1 2 3 4   5   6 7 8 9 10 11 12 13 14 15 16 17 18

Transfer your score totals to this matrix by shading each row in relation to the total score for that influence source. This will provide you with the relative strength of each of your currencies of influence and its relationship to the other sources of influence.

EXHIBIT 8.

Currencies of Influence (32)

A number of studies have been conducted to compare the effects of using different sources of influence. Most of these studies have used influence measures based on the power typology proposed by researchers French and Raven. The seven generally accepted sources of influence are Tyrannical Influence, Networking and Alliance Influence, All-Knowing Guru Influence, Informational Influence, Pecking Order Influence, Charismatic Influence, and Midas Influence.

Tyrannical Influence   is based on absolute tyrannical control, force, and fear. Scoring high in this currency is seen as forcing compliance and obedience to your wishes. Failure to obey usually leads to punishment, such as undesirable work assignments, reprimands, exclusion from opportunities and information, limited mobility, and the like. With coercion there is no chance of gaining real commitment from colleagues. Colleagues typically react to coercion with physical withdrawal (absenteeism, quit), psychological withdrawal (noncommunicativeness, alcoholism, drugs), or hostility and aggression (theft, slowdowns, sabotage).

Networking and Alliance Influence   is based on contacts (connections) within the organization—or even outside the organization. Scoring high in networking influence forces colleagues to comply since they want to gain the favor or avoid the wrath of your powerful connections. Managers who have connection power can get others to do things because they can promise a link or an "in" with important people.

All-Knowing Guru Influence   is based on providing uncommon expertise, experience, knowledge, and so forth. Scoring high in this currency is viewed as having the expertise and technical competence to directly influence the work behavior of less qualified and knowledgeable colleagues. Expertise works because others often need skills and knowledge to expedite their goal attainment.

Informational Influence   is based on possession of or direct access to information that is perceived as valuable and needed by others. Scoring high in information power means you have the capability to work through others by promising access to data, thus letting colleagues in on things.

Pecking Order Influence is based on an individual's or group's actual position on the organizational chart and its concomitant right to be obeyed. Such a position gives the manager who occupies it control over others because of the chain-of-command nature of the "slot" in the hierarchy. Scoring high in pecking order influence demands compliance since colleagues feel this individual has the right to expect obedience and compliance.

Charismatic Influence is based on one's personal magnetism, charisma, and dynamic personality. Scoring high in charismatic influence means you are generally respected and admired by colleagues. Your dynamic, magnetic personality itself greatly influences others. This currency of influence can take such forms as a sense of high standards, dynamic speaking ability, willingness to sacrifice oneself to principles, and capability for helping ordinary people achieve extraordinary results.

Midas Influence is based on one's ability to provide both tangible and intangible rewards. A manager perceived as scoring high in Midas influence can motivate others because the prospect of positive recompense is envisioned. Rewards can be tangible, such as salary increases, awards, promotions—or intangible, such as verbal recognition and praise.

(Adapted from J. R. French, Jr., and B. Raven, "The Basis of Social Power." In *Studies in Social Power*, ed. D. Cartwright. Ann Arbor: University of Michigan Press, 1959.)

EXHIBIT 9.
Writer's Digest (46)

Writer's Digest

Phrases That Dazzle:
- professional balance   - organizational tick
- passion for excellence   - access provider
- pockets of loyalty   - highly responsive
- organizational scaffolding   teams
- smell of innovation   - confrontational
- corporate cultures   leadership
- dinosaur management   - corporate wrappers
- learning laboratory   - basher of protocol
- excess provider   - corporate fabric
- value shaping

Quotes:

"The very essence of leadership is (that) you
have to have a vision. It's got to be a
vision you articulate clearly + forcefully on
every occasion. You can't blow an
uncertain trumpet."
          (Father Theodore Hesburgh, former President
               Notre Dame Univ.)

"Has the leader a right to mold + shape?
Of what use is aging, experience, + wisdom
if not to be the leaver for those who
are younger? Of what use is pain if not
to teach others to avoid it? The leader
not only has the right; if he is a leader,
he has the obligation."
          (Harry Levinson in The Exceptional Executive)

EXHIBIT 10.
Communication Competence (47)

The major focus of this checklist is to help you increase the communication options at your disposal, so that you can choose the most appropriate alternative for any situation you encounter. The more strategies you have available, the more flexible you are in reacting and responding. Enhancing your repertoire of interpersonal communication skills is important to productive, rewarding interpersonal work relationships. You can increase awareness of your everyday communication behavior, generate alternatives, and thereby increase the size and variety of your communication expertise. As a result, you will be a more competent communicator, a manager who can benefit from a relationship in ways that are mutually acceptable.

To get a better idea of your interpersonal communication competence at this point, respond to the statements below as they relate to your communication behavior. Consult this checklist often to sharpen your interpersonal skills:

	YES	NO
1. I use appropriate eye contact when conversing.	___	___
2. I refer to the other person and the relationship existing between us.	___	___
3. I nod my head at appropriate times while the other person is talking.	___	___
4. I maintain a relaxed, controlled speaking rate.	___	___
5. I smile appropriately when I am conversing.	___	___
6. I acknowledge that my perceptions of the other person are my reality, not his or hers.	___	___
7. I remain comfortably close to the person with whom I am speaking.	___	___
8. I am relaxed and have a comfortable posture.	___	___
9. I don't hesitate or use many vocal pauses (uh, you know, etc.) when I talk.	___	___
10. I avoid playing with objects such as a pen, paper, or silverware.	___	___

		YES	NO
11.	When the other person smiles at me, I return the smile.	——	——
12.	I indicate that I understand what the other person is saying and feeling.	——	——
13.	I show that I am listening by using verbal reinforcers (I see, Go on, Uh huh, Right).	——	——
14.	I avoid unnecessarily interrupting the other person.	——	——
15.	I make sure that we both have an opportunity to talk and that the conversation flows without too many silent pauses.	——	——
16.	I use appropriate gestures (hand movements) when I talk.	——	——
17.	I don't play with my hair or my clothing during conversations.	——	——
18.	I avoid frequent and lengthy pauses when I converse.	——	——
19.	I generally control the beginning and end of the encounter and the topics discussed.	——	——
20.	I listen intently, giving my undivided attention.	——	——

EXHIBIT 11.

Interpersonal Encounter Expectations Check (47)

Carl Rogers, an eminent humanistic psychologist and author of *On Becoming a Person,* asks himself these questions as he makes contact with another person. His goal is to enter into a helping relationship, whether it be with clients, students, colleagues, friends, or family. This introspection applies to managers, too, so ask yourself these same questions in your dealings with co-workers:

1. How can I *be* in some way that will be perceived by the other person as trustworthy, dependable, or consistent in some deep sense?
2. How can I be expressive enough as a person that what I am will be communicated unambiguously?
3. How can I let myself experience positive attitudes toward this other person—attitudes of warmth, caring, liking, interest, respect?
4. How can I be strong enough as a person to be separate from others? How can I respect my own feelings, my own needs, as well as co-workers? How can I own and, if need be, express my own feelings as something belonging to me and separate from the feelings of another?
5. Am I secure enough within myself to permit someone else his or her separateness? How can I permit others to be what they are— honest or deceitful, infantile or adult, despairing or overconfident? How can I give them the freedom to *be?*
6. How can I step into another's private world so completely that I lose all desire to evaluate or judge it. How can I enter in more sensitively and move about in it freely, without trampling on meanings that are precious to someone else? How can I sense it so accurately that I can catch not only the meanings of another's experience that are obvious, but also those meanings that are seen only dimly or as confusion?
7. How can I receive others as they are? How can I communicate this attitude positively (nonjudgmentally)?
8. In what ways can I act with sufficient sensitivity in work relation-

ships that my behavior will not be perceived as a threat? In what ways can I choose to be less confrontive?

9. How can I free others from the threat of external evaluation?
10. How can I meet other individuals as people who, like I am, are *becoming* better people?

(Adapted from C. Rogers, *On Becoming a Person*. Boston: Houghton-Mifflin Co., 1961.)

EXHIBIT 12.

Conflict Styles Questionnaire (50)

Each question contains two statements that describe how people deal with conflict. Distribute five points between the two statements for each question. The statement more like the way you would respond should receive the higher number of points. (This assessment is adapted from R. Kilmann and K. Thomas's "Interpersonal Conflict-handling Inventory," *Psychological Reports,* Vol. 37, 1975.)

For example, if reaction A strongly describes your behavior,

_5_ a.

_0_ b.

However, if a and b are both characteristic, but b is a little more characteristic of your behavior than a,

_2_ a.

_3_ b.

1. ___ a. I am most comfortable letting others take responsibility for solving a problem.
   ___ b. Rather than negotiate differences, I stress those points upon which agreement is obvious.
2. ___ a. I pride myself in finding compromise solutions.
   ___ b. I examine all the issues involved in any disagreement.
3. ___ a. I usually persist in pursuing my side of an issue.
   ___ b. I prefer to soothe others' feelings and preserve relationships.
4. ___ a. I pride myself in finding compromise solutions.
   ___ b. I usually sacrifice my wishes for the wishes of a colleague.
5. ___ a. I consistently seek a colleague's help in solution-finding.
   ___ b. I do whatever is necessary to avoid tension.

6. ___ a. As a rule, I avoid dealing with conflict.

___ b. I defend my position and push my views.

7. ___ a. I postpone dealing with conflict until I have had some time to think it over.

___ b. I am willing to give up some points if others give up some too.

8. ___ a. I use my influence to have my views accepted.

___ b. I attempt to get all concerns and issues immediately out in the open.

9. ___ a. I feel that most differences are not worth worrying about.

___ b. I make a strong effort to get my way on issues I care about.

10. ___ a. Occasionally I use my authority or technical knowledge to get my way.

___ b. I prefer compromise solution to problems.

11. ___ a. I believe that a group can reach a better solution than any one person can working independently.

___ b. I often defer to the wishes of others.

12. ___ a. I usually avoid taking positions that would create controversy.

___ b. I'm willing to give a little if a colleague will give a little, too.

13. ___ a. I generally propose middle ground as a solution.

___ b. I consistently press to "sell" my viewpoint.

14. ___ a. I prefer to hear everyone's side of an issue before making judgments.

___ b. I demonstrate the logic and benefits of my position.

15. ___ a. I would rather give in than argue about trivialities.

___ b. I avoid being "put on the spot."

16. ___ a. I refuse to hurt a colleague's feelings.

___ b. I will defend my rights as a group member.

17. ___ a. I am usually firm in pursuing my point of view.

___ b. I'll walk away from disagreements before someone gets hurt.

18. ___ a. If it makes colleagues happy, I will agree with them.

_____ b. I believe that give-and-take is the best way to resolve any disagreement.

19. _____ a. I prefer to have everyone involved in a conflict generate alternatives together.

_____ b. When the group is discussing a serious problem, I usually keep quiet.

20. _____ a. I would rather openly resolve conflict than conceal differences.

_____ b. I seek ways to balance gains and losses for equitable solutions.

21. _____ a. In problem solving, I am usually considerate of colleagues' viewpoints.

_____ b. I prefer a direct and objective discussion of any disagreement.

22. _____ a. I seek solutions that meet some of everyone's needs.

_____ b. I will argue as long as necessary to get my position heard.

23. _____ a. I like to assess the problem and identify a mutually agreeable solution.

_____ b. When people challenge my position, I simply ignore them.

24. _____ a. If colleagues feel strongly about a position, I defer to it even if I don't agree.

_____ b. I am willing to settle for a compromise solution.

25. _____ a. I am very persuasive when I have to be to win in a conflict situation.

_____ b. I believe in the saying, "Kill your enemies with kindness."

26. _____ a. I will bargain with colleagues in an effort to manage disagreement.

_____ b. I listen attentively before expressing my views.

27. _____ a. I avoid taking controversial positions.

_____ b. I'm willing to give up my position for the benefit of the group.

28. _____ a. I enjoy competitive situations and "play" hard to win.

_____ b. Whenever possible, I seek out knowledgeable colleagues to help resolve disagreements.

29. _____ a. I will surrender some of my demands, but I have to get something in return.

_____ b. I don't like to air differences and usually keep my concerns to myself.

30. _____ a. I generally avoid hurting a colleague's feelings.

_____ b. When a colleague and I disagree, I prefer to bring the issue out into the open so we can discuss it.

Conflict Styles Response Summary

3A ___	2A ___	1A ___	1B ___	2B ___
6B ___	4A ___	5B ___	3B ___	5A ___
8A ___	7B ___	6A ___	4B ___	8B ___
9B ___	10B ___	7A ___	11B ___	11A ___
10A ___	12B ___	9A ___	15A ___	14A ___
13B ___	13A ___	12A ___	16A ___	19A ___
14B ___	18B ___	15B ___	18A ___	20A ___
16B ___	20B ___	17B ___	21A ___	21B ___
17A ___	22A ___	19B ___	24A ___	23A ___
22B ___	24B ___	23B ___	25B ___	26B ___
25A ___	26A ___	27A ___	27B ___	28B ___
28A ___	29A ___	29B ___	30A ___	30B ___
TOTAL ___	TOTAL ___	TOTAL ___	TOTAL ___	TOTAL ___

Plot your scores on the graph below:

	Total	0	10	20	30	40	50	60
Competing	___		†	†	†	†	†	
Compromising	___		†	†	†	†	†	
Avoiding	___		†	†	†	†	†	
Accommodating	___		†	†	†	†	†	
Collaborating	___		†	†	†	†	†	
		0	10	20	30	40	50	60

EXHIBIT 13.

Assessing Your Conflict Management Styles (50)

Questions to Ask Yourself

1. How do the questionnaire results compare with my perception of how I manage disagreement and resolve conflict?
2. Based on my profile, what are my strengths and weaknesses? Dominant conflict-management style?
3. As I recollect, what are some specific instances when I have successfully resolved conflict?
4. My unsuccessful attempts to manage disagreement are usually characterized by what types of behavior?
5. In what ways do I allow the slings and arrows hurled at me to become walls of confinement or immobilizing stings?
6. If I am able to accept within my own mind all the possible responses to conflict, what place might compassion hold in resolving value differences?
7. Respond thoughtfully to this statement: "Conflict isn't negative, it just is."
8. Nature uses conflict as its primary motivator for change (creating beautiful beaches, canyons, mountains, and pearls). How can I harness its energies to create a more synergistic landscape at work?
9. How can I use what I have discovered about the differences in conflict-management styles to choreograph team support at work?
10. Internalize this statement by Will Rogers: "Why not go out on a limb? That's where the fruit is."

EXHIBIT 14.
Conflict Management Styles (50)

There are five generally accepted styles for dealing with conflict issues: avoidance, accommodation, collaboration, compromise, and competition.[1] Nothing is inherently right or wrong with any of these styles. Each can be appropriate and most effective, depending on the situation, issues to resolve, and personalities involved. Let's take a closer look at each of the styles:

- *Competing* is an aggressive and totally antagonistic style. A "competitor" pursues his or her own views at a colleague's expense. This is a power-oriented mode in which a group member uses whatever means seem appropriate to win. Competing could mean "standing up for your rights," defending a position which you believe is correct, or demonstrating a no-holds-barred, win-at-all-costs attitude.
- *Accommodating* is an unassertive, self-sacrificing, and hospitable style that is in direct opposition to competing. Colleagues who use this approach relinquish their own concerns to satisfy the concerns of another employee. Accommodating usually takes the form of selfless generosity or blind obedience and yielding completely to another's point of view.
- *Avoiding* is an unassertive, side-stepping, and retreat-oriented conflict management style. An "avoider" generally chooses to dodge conflict at all costs. Avoiding might take the form of diplomatically side-stepping an issue, postponing an issue until a better time, or simply withdrawing from a threatening situation (emotionally, physically, or intellectually).
- *Collaborating* is a (more) cooperative, synergistic, multilateral conflict resolution style. Collaborators find mutually satisfying solutions. They dig into an issue to identify underlying issues and find mutually satisfying Band-Aids or remedies. Collaboration involves demonstrating musketeer-like team focus, agreeing not to compete for resources, and using confrontation to find creative solutions to mutually engaging problems.
- *Compromising* involves finding expedient, mutually acceptable solutions that partially satisfy both parties. Compromising means that

---

[1] Kilmann, R., and K. Thomas, "Interpersonal Conflict-handling Behavior As Reflections of Jungian Personality Dimensions. *Psychological Reports* 37 (1975), 971–980.

both parties "split the difference" in order to settle disagreements. It might mean exchanging concessions, or seeking quick, middle-ground solutions.

Each of these conflict styles is an effective approach to conflict resolution if used appropriately. Conflict is characterized by different degrees of volatility that require a different conflict-management style to handle discord, clashes, or disputes. Once managers discover how a particular conflict-management style affects their ability to resolve conflict, the art of creative fighting becomes a powerful people-moving skill.

EXHIBIT 15.

Procrastination Profile (62)

Projects/Situations or People	"Rational Lies" Habitually Used	My Reward for Overcoming Procrastination
Completing budget	Gather data to extreme; get that third cup of coffee	Finish Budget → Buy a new blouse or tie
Discuss absenteeism with John or Jane	Collect data; make excuses; do paperwork	Have meeting → Dine out at favorite restaurant

EXHIBIT 16.

Bantamweight or Heavyweight? (68)

Assigning weights to different goals is an evaluation method often used to legitimize priorities. The basic procedure for most weighting methods is to generate a list of evaluation criteria, assign weights to the criteria, rate each previously screened goal against the criteria, and then select the goals that best satisfy the requirements of the criteria. The steps in this weighting scheme:

1. Using the Referee's Choice Weighting Sheet, list all the criteria used to evaluate the ideas in the column marked *Criteria*.
2. Use the list of criteria found in the *Criteria* column or add some of your own.
3. In the column marked *Importance*, numerically rate the relative importance of each criterion on a scale from 1 (least important) to 5 (most important).
4. In the column marked *Level of Conformance*, numerically rate the degree to which each goal conforms to each criterion on a scale from 1 (minimum level of conformance to criterion) to 5 (meets criterion very well).
5. Multiply the values assigned to the *Importance* measurement with the values assigned to the *Level of Conformance* measurement. Record the score in the subtotal column next to the *Criterion* measurement for that particular goal.
6. Total the products obtained for each goal and write the score in the *Weighted Totals* column.
7. Examine the scores and rank-order the goals according to their numerical alignment with the mission statement. The higher the score, the higher the alignment. Give top priority to the goal with the highest weighted value.

Referee's Choice Weighting Sheet

MISSION STATEMENT:

PERFORMANCE GOAL STATEMENTS

CRITERIA	IMPOR-TANCE	GOAL: LEVEL OF CONFOR-MANCE	SUB-TOTAL	GOAL: LEVEL OF CONFOR-MANCE	SUB-TOTAL	GOAL: LEVEL OF CONFOR-MANCE	SUB-TOTAL	GOAL: LEVEL OF CONFOR-MANCE	SUB-TOTAL	GOAL: LEVEL OF CONFOR-MANCE	SUB-TOTAL	GOAL: LEVEL OF CONFOR-MANCE	SUB-TOTAL
Profitability													
Practicality													
Compatibility with Strategic Plan													
Management Support													
Ease of Implementation													
Human Resource Availability													
Material/Equipment Availability													
Marketability													
Cost Effectiveness													
Urgency													
Maintainability													
Organizationwide Support													
Weighted Totals													

EXHIBIT 17.

Activity versus Accomplishment (68)

After you have a set of weighted goals or objectives you believe in (derived from previous weighting and screening techniques) determine whether you are confusing activity with accomplishment. This sobering technique is an excellent eye-opener. It'll help you align what you've promised to do with what you're actually doing. The procedure is simple. The reality testing is precise and immediate. The steps in realizing the immense benefits of this exceptional technique are as follows:

1. Write your organization's mission statement in the space provided at the top of the decision matrix.
2. Record the goal and objective statements already arrived at during previous screenings.
3. Copy the previously assigned weights in the space provided for each goal and objective statement.
4. List the projects you are currently involved in on a day-to-day basis.
5. Consider the relevance each project has to each of the goals and objectives you've identified as important. Numerically rate how relevant each project is using the following rating scale:

   0—Not relevant at all (compost material)
   1—Not sure how it relates (apples and oranges)
   3—Some parts of it relate (rinds and seeds)
   5—Most of it relates (juice or pulp)
   10—Absolute and direct alignment (ham and eggs relationship)

6. Add the assigned weights and relevance scores to obtain the priority score for each project. Record the weighted sum in the far right column.
7. Rank-order the projects according to score, assigning the highest priority to the highest score.
8. Consider modifying, combining, eliminating, adapting, miniaturizing, or substituting those projects that were assigned the lowest ratings.

Activity versus Accomplishment Decision Matrix

MISSION STATEMENT:

Projects / *Assigned Weights* / Goals/Objectives								Priority Score

EXHIBIT 18.
Chain of Service (75)

Using this chart, fill in specific names for each category (names of companies, vendors, distributors, the public). Determine your location and your department's location in the chain of service so that you can quickly spot your link in the chain. You may find members of your department represented in more than one link. Be as specific as possible. Remember, the external customer is *anyone* outside your company who uses your service or product. The internal customer is anyone *inside* your company who benefits from your service or product.

> **External Customers**
>
>
>

> **Individuals/Departments Who Have Direct Contact with External Customers**
>
>
>

> **Individuals/Departments Providing Support to Groups Listed Above**
>
>
>

EXHIBIT **19.**

Let the Manager Out:
An Intensive Developmental Journal
(Sample Journal Entries) (76)

DAILY LOG

Date: Entry #
Entry:

INTERPERSONAL EXPERIENCES
[Persons who have had the most impact (positive and negative) on my professional
career—insights gained, changes made, growth in process.]

Date: Entry #
Entry:

GROUP EXPERIENCES
[Groups—inside and outside of work—that have revitalized me, changed me,
deepened me]

Date: Entry #
Entry:

LIFE-CHANGING EVENTS AND CIRCUMSTANCES
[Noteworthy events, situations, circumstances that have shaped my professional career]

Date: Entry #
Event/Circumstance:

DIALOGUE WITH MY BODY
[What is my body saying to me? In what ways have I taken care of it? Abused it?
Overextended it? Polluted it?]

Date: Entry #
Entry:

DREAMS, SERENDIPITOUS EXPERIENCES, HIGHLY CREATIVE MOMENTS
[Times in my life when special messages have come to guide me]

Date: Entry #
Entry:

CROSS-ROADS
[Paths taken and not taken]

Date: Entry #
Path Taken/Not taken:

THOUGHTS ABOUT TOMORROW
[Tomorrow's aspirations; challenges; emotional, intellectual, or spiritual growth;
expectations; fears; desires; professional outlook]

Date: Entry #
Entry:

EXHIBIT 20.

Professional Skills Inventory: A Self-Assessment (80)

Directions   For each skill, indicate, in the appropriate column, if you use it in your current job, if you've used it previously (in other jobs, volunteer work, and so forth), or if you've never had an opportunity to use it.

For those skills you have used, rate your assessment of your performance according to the scale provided. Force yourself to spread your rankings out, so that you have a combination of all five ratings.

After you have completed the inventory, ask yourself these questions:

- What pattern is there in my strong skills? In my weak skills?
- How do my skills compare with the requirements of the positions I am exploring?
- What areas do I need to strengthen? How can I do it?

**Performance
Rating Scale:**   5 = Outstanding Skill   2 = Not a Strong Skill
                     4 = Fairly Strong Skill   1 = Weak in This Skill
                     3 = Average Skill

Skill	Use This Currently	Have Used Previously	Have Never Used	Performance (1–5 point scale)
Handles variety of tasks				
Follows instructions				
Resolves problems				
Makes good use of resources				
Communicates verbally				
Communicates in writing				

(continued)

Skill	Use This Currently	Have Used Previously	Have Never Used	Performance (1–5 point scale)
Plans and organizes work				
Manages time				
Anticipates problems				
Sets realistic goals				
Works within budget guidelines				
Cooperates with others				
Listens to others				
Resolves conflict				
Demonstrates persuasiveness				
Makes decisions				
Demonstrates creativity				
Delegates				
Accepts responsibility				
Conducts meetings				
Understands organizational politics				
Manages multiple priorities				
Keeps supervisor informed				
Takes risks				
Motivates others				
Takes initiative				
Uses facts and figures				
Supervises others				

Skill	Use This Currently	Have Used Previously	Have Never Used	Performance (1–5 point scale)
Handles stress				
Makes formal presentations				
Repairs machinery				
Operates equipment				
Analyzes data				
Follows directions				
Is flexible and adaptable				
Applies past experience				
Makes sound judgments				
Stays current in profession				
Asks good questions				
Gives good feedback				
Clarifies expectations				
Encourages cooperation				
Is open to criticism				
Sees big picture				
Plans well strategically				
Plans well tactically				
Gives constructive feedback				
Deals easily with complexity				
Uses common sense				
Promotes quality				

(continued)

Skill	Use This Currently	Have Used Previously	Have Never Used	Performance (1–5 point scale)
Respects individual differences				
Sets high standards				
Operates computers				
Advocates teamwork				
Sells ideas				
Challenges tradition				
Defends policy				
Handles customer complaints				
Uses telephone				
Provides customer service				
Sells products or services				
Reexamines outmoded assumptions				

EXHIBIT 21.
Thirteen Dream Appreciation Hints (84)

There are symbols in dreams for the same reason that there are figures of speech in poetry and slang in everyday life.   Calvin Hall

1. Recognize that every dream is sent to offer the dreamer help, health, and happiness.
2. Walk the mystical path with practical feet. Interpret dreams literally first by examining signs of objective truths such as warnings, reminders, health issues, and so forth. Then consider metaphorical and symbolical interpretations.
3. Consider the relationship of each dream theme to some event or preoccupation of the previous day or two (called day residue).
4. Analyze the emotional tone of the dream and its relationship to one's current life dramas.
5. Realize that recurrent dream themes may have different meanings depending on where one is in consciousness at the time of the dream.
6. Recognize that dreams come to expand and transform us, not to diminish us or frighten us.
7. Believe that the best interpreter of your dreams is yourself—your own unfailing guru within.
8. Realize that dreams are as real as one's waking life.
9. Appreciate the fact that each dream has several levels of meaning.
10. Recognize that a series of dreams that occur during the same night often has a unifying theme.
11. Nightmares usually indicate poor or inadequate diet. They are also psychic "awakeners" that direct you to clean up your act—now.
12. Look for past life experiences in your dreams. Usually they become manifest in color and appear with the proper attire of the era. They warn against repeating the same old mistakes or hanging on to the same outdated attitudes or beliefs.
13. Do not fear conversations with those who have died. If the communication is one-sided, it may denote telepathy. Dialogues may suggest actual transpersonal or cosmic encounters.

EXHIBIT 22.

Fourteen Basic Dream Recall Hints (84)

No single theory can do justice to the richness of dreams, and one very simple fact about them—which almost all psychotherapists neglect completely—is their direct relation to the events and thoughts of the previous day.   Ann Faraday

1. A conscious commitment and desire to remember one's dreams is probably the single most important step in dream recall.
2. Decide what means you will use to record your dreams and place everything you need next to where you are sleeping. The more convenient and accessible your recording materials and devices are, the easier it will be for you to record your dreams.
3. Establish presleep incubation rituals.
4. If you awaken during a dream, immediately record a few key words or images. Procrastination is a thief in the night.
5. If you do not recall any dreams upon awakening, move into habitual sleeping positions and dialogue with your dreaming mind.
6. If dream recall is difficult, visualize some of the faces of people you have strong emotional responses to in waking life.
7. Join a dream appreciation group. Attend dream workshops.
8. Add B-complex vitamins to your diet.
9. Repression of repugnant dream material too intense or disturbing is shoved into our transpersonal storehouse for future integration. Therefore, some highly emotionally charged content may not surface until the dreamer is psychodynamically ready.
10. Before drifting to sleep, visualize yourself waking in the morning and remembering clearly several dreams or dream fragments.
11. Keep a Dream Diary.
12. Read articles about dreams, listen to audiocassettes, watch TV shows and documentaries about dreams. (An interest in mysticism, meditation, psychoanalysis, or hypnosis will also help unlock the dream gates.)
13. Eliminate life-style saboteurs of dream recall such as late night eating, alcoholic beverages, sleeping pills, poor or inadequate diet.
14. Confront unrealistic fears and expectations about the nature of the dream content. Recognize that sexual fantasies, uncharacteristic behavior, and dreams of death are common themes.

EXHIBIT 23.

Dream Bibliography (84)

Bonime, Walter. *The Clinical Use of Dreams*. New York: Basic Books, Inc., 1961.

Dee, N. *The Dreamer's Workbook*. Wellingborough, Northamptonshire, England: Woolnough Bookbinding Ltd., 1989.

Faraday, Ann. *Dream Power*. New York: Berkley Books, 1972.

French, Thomas, and Erika Fromm. *Dream Interpretation: A New Approach*. New York: Basic Books, Inc., 1964.

Freud, Sigmund. *The Interpretation of Dreams* (new trans. by James Strachey). London: George Allen & Unwin, 1954, 1961. New York: Basic Books, Inc., 1955.

Fromm, Erich. *The Forgotten Language: An Introduction to the Understanding of Dreams, Fairytales & Myths*. New York: Holt, Rinehart and Winston, 1951.

Green, Celia. *Lucid Dreams*. Oxford: Institute of Psychophysical Research, 1968.

Gutheil, E. *The Handbook of Dream Analysis*. New York: Liveright Publishing, 1979.

Hall, Calvin S. *The Meaning of Dreams*. New York: McGraw-Hill Book Co., 1953.

Hartmann, Ernest, ed. *Sleep and Dreaming*. Boston: Little, Brown & Co., 1970. London: Churchill, 1970.

Kramer, Milton, ed. *Dream Psychology and the New Biology of Dreaming*. Springfield, IL: Charles C. Thomas, 1969.

Luce, Gay Baer, and Julius Segal. *Sleep*. New York: Coward-McCann, 1966.

Mackenzie, Norman. *Dreams and Dreaming*. London: Aldus Books, 1965.

May, Rolo. *The Courage to Create*. New York: Bantam Books, 1975.

Oswald, Ian. *Sleeping and Waking*. New York: Elsevier Publishing Co., 1962.

Ullman, M., and N. Zimmerman. *Working with Dreams*. New York: St. Martin's Press, 1979.

Van de Castle, Robert L. *The Psychology of Dreaming*. New York: General Learning Corporation, 1971.

Von Grunebaum, G. E., and Roger Caillois. *The Dream and Human Societies*. Berkeley: University of California Press, 1966.

EXHIBIT 24.

Pendulum of Light (85)

- Adjourn to a quiet place that offers peace and solitude.
- Sit in a comfortable position in which your back can be held straight without straining.
- Close your eyes and inhale slowly through your nostrils. With each long, slow exhalation, imagine you *see* the tension flowing out of your body from your head and falling *south* into your toes. Do this for a few minutes until you feel relaxed and comfortable.
- Let your breathing settle down naturally to its own pace.
- Now imagine that you have a beam of white light extending from your center through the top of your head. Picture your center as being about the size of a baseball.
- Let the light beam, emanating from your center, begin to grow until it fills your entire body. Expand it to include the area around your head and body. Let your breathing be easy, relaxed, and rhythmic.
- Begin swaying back and forth for fifteen to twenty seconds to establish a natural rhythm, let the swing and your cocoon of light become half as large as before. Continue swaying with the same rhythm, but decrease the swing proportionately to the size of your "new" smaller, but brighter center.
- Continue decreasing the side-to-side rotation of your swing and the size of your center.
- Soon your body will cease to sway. It may be more difficult to picture the actual size of your center. Simply focus your attention on an inner sense of or picture of your center diminishing to an infinitesimal size. The vibratory quality of the swinging pendulum of light that follows a single, infinitely decreasing point becomes the focus of your attention now. This pendulum of light becomes your psychic elevator and allows you a comfortable ride inward to the source of your being.
- When extraneous thoughts come into your mind, do not fight them. Instead, easily come back to that vibratory quality of the center, which is becoming smaller, smaller—still smaller—and again, still diminishing. The vibratory quality may be perceived differently and may change periodically throughout its inner journey. You may perceive it as a feeling, a sound, or an image. Allow it to take whatever form it chooses. Trust its wisdom.
- Continue this process for ten to fifteen minutes. Become one with the spark of light. Bathe in the light. Feel protected by the light. Trans-

formed by it. Accepted by it. Honored by it. Empowered by its brilliance. Revitalized and refreshed by its constancy. Loved by it. Now bring your awareness back to your breathing and breathe deeply into each and every area of your body. Take a few moments to do this; don't hurry. Now bring your awareness back into your body and the immediate surroundings. Welcome back to a new, more revitalized, and connected you.

EXHIBIT **25.**

Multiple Listings (91)

Each of the following lists is recommended as an introspective launch site. Spend quality time on each list. Start anywhere, but be sure to complete all fifty-two Multiple Listings.

101 Things I Believe In
101 Things I Do Well
101 Things I'd Like to Know
    More About

101 Things I Could Learn from Children
101 Things I Could Learn from Nature
101 Reasons to Stay Physically Fit
101 Accomplishments I'm Proud Of
101 Things I'd Do If I Took Time To Do Them
101 Things I Want to Accomplish
    in the Next Twelve Months

101 Things I'm Thankful For
101 Ways I Sabotage My Success
101 Things That Are Going Right
101 Things That Derail Me
101 Things That Once Frightened Me,
    but Don't Anymore
101 Doubts I Am Having Right Now
101 Things I've Done Before (but Haven't
    Done in a While) That I'd Like to Do Again

101 Sacrifices I've Made
101 Ways to Motivate People at Work
101 Ways I Can Make a Living
101 Concerns about Being Wealthy
101 Ways I Help and Support Others
101 Things I Value at Work
101 Things That Really Motivate Me
101 Things I Value in Life
101 Talents and Abilities I Use
101 Talents and Abilities I Wish I Had
101 Extraordinary People Who
    Have Died

101 Famous People I'd Like to Meet
101 Things I'd Save If My House
     Caught Fire

101 Things I Haven't Finished
101 Things I Won't Do Again
101 Principles to Live By
101 Things That Have Made Me
     Shed a Few Tears

101 Possessions I'm Tired Of
101 Responsibilities I Wouldn't Want to Have
101 Things That Make Me Laugh or Smile
101 Ways I'm Selfish
101 Things I Get Angry About
101 Places I'd Like to Visit or Live In
101 Rules or Laws I've Broken
101 Feelings I'm Capable of Expressing
101 Fantasies I'd Be Too Embarrassed
     to Make Public

101 Ways I Could Improve Myself
101 Things I'd Like to Tell My Family
101 Adjectives I Could Use
     to Describe Myself

101 Things I'd Do If I Only Had
     One Year to Live

101 Decisions Other People
     Have Made for Me

101 Improvements I'd Make at Work
101 Places I Wouldn't Want to Visit
     or Live In

101 Ways to Achieve World Peace
101 Inventions That Make Life Easier
101 Strategies to Reduce or
     Eliminate Stress

(Adapted from "A List of 100" in Kathleen Adams, *Journal to the Self*. New York: Warner Books, 1990.)

EXHIBIT 26.
Laundry List (93)

This exceptional solution-finding technique uses categories of questions that generate ideas of how something can be modified to arrive at novel and innovative uses. Based on problem-delineation checklists used by Taylor,[1] Osborn,[2] Davis and Scott,[3] Davis et al.,[4] it integrates functional characteristics of movement, in general, and asks seven key questions relating to simulation, magnification, miniaturization, substitution, alignment, contradiction, and combination. Sample questions:

1. Alignment   In what ways can the structure or composition of this product or service be altered?

2. Combination   What existing materials, processes, roles, or functions could be combined to create a unique solution?

3. Contradiction   What would the opposite function of this product or service look like?

4. Magnification   What could be added to this product or service?

5. Miniaturization   What could be taken away from this product or service?

6. Simulation   What other product or service is similar to this one?

7. Substitution   What could be used in the place of this service or in place of a portion of this product?

[1] Taylor, J. W., *How to Create Ideas* (Englewood Cliffs, NJ: Scribner, 1963).
[2] Osborn, A. F., *Applied Imagination* 3d ed. (Englewood Cliffs, NJ: Scribner, 1963).
[3] Davis, G. A., and J. A. Scott, eds., *Training Creative Thinking* (Huntington, NY: Krieger, 1978).
[4] Davis, G. A., W. E. Roweton, A. J. Train, T. R. Warren, and S. E. Houtman, *Laboratory Studies of Creative Thinking Techniques: The Checklist and Morphological Synthesis Methods*, Technical Report No. 94, Wisconsin Research and Development Center for Cognitive Learning, University of Wisconsin, 1969.

Steps to use to maximize this technique:

1. State problem.
2. Use all of the seven sets of laundry lists to generate ideas.
3. Evaluate solutions—determine their relevance, novelty, and application as viable solutions.
4. Another level of novelty could be attained by combining the outputs of two or more sets of categories and establishing new linkages.

Alignment

account	clean	foam	iodize
address	clog	fold	ionize
adjust	coast	fracture	jackknife
administer	comb	gauge	jettison
aerate	compute	girdle	jockey
aggravate	control	govern	juggle
agitate	convalesce	grade	jump
align	crank	grill	knock
alphabetize	creep	groove	lance
analyze	curl	guide	leak
anchor	cushion	gut	legalize
angle	dedicate	hammer	legitimate
arc	deliver	hang	level
bake	demand	haul	lick
bathe	dial	heave	liquify
beat	distribute	herd	list
bend	diverge	hijack	load
bevel	drag	hurl	loop
bind	drill	hurdle	loose
blister	dynamite	hurry	lower
blow	edit	hyphenate	lunge
boil	elasticize	immerse	mail
bounce	even	immigrate	manage
brush	extend	immunize	map
calculate	fence	incline	marginate
carry	file	ingest	materialize
caulk	filter	inoculate	metabolize
certify	fire	insulate	microwave
chap	fish	interfold	migrate
chase	flee	interpenetrate	moderate
chill	floss	investigate	modernize

mold	recoil	sit	tamp
monitor	recover	skid	tantalize
navigate	recuperate	slant	tap
negotiate	redirect	slip	tease
normalize	reel	smelt	tenderize
numb	refrigerate	smooth	throw
obligate	refurbish	snuggle	tickle
orchestrate	regenerate	soften	tighten
order	regiment	solidify	tip
organize	regulate	sort	torque
oscillate	reheat	spear	tote
outstrip	relax	spin	tour
park	relay	square	tow
pass	relocate	squash	transfer
pause	remain	stabilize	transmigrate
percolate	remit	stack	transmute
permeate	repair	stamp	transplant
pile	repress	stash	transport
pipe	rest	steam	trill
pound	retreat	steer	tuck
press	roast	step	tune
probe	roll	sterilize	turn
protect	rotate	stick	twirl
pry	sail	stiffen	unfold
pull	sanitize	stock	uproot
quench	scatter	store	vaccinate
quiz	screen	straighten	vent
rack	scroll	string	vibrate
rake	seat	surf	wash
rank	secure	swallow	wave
ransack	sequence	sweep	whip
rate	settle	swirl	whirl
ream	shift	swoop	wiggle
recess	shuffle	syringe	wrinkle
reclaim	shunt	tackle	zoom
recline	simplify	tame	

Combination

access
accommodate
acidify
adapt
adhere
adjoin
affix
alternate
assess
associate
balance
blend
bolt
bond
brace
braid
bridge
button
catalog
catch
cement
channel
check
clap
clip
club
coat
coax
coil
collate
commit
compose
compound
concentrate
contact
contract
convolute
coordinate
curve
depend
engage

escort
fan
farm
fasten
feed
float
fluorinate
flush
fortify
fuse
gas
glaze
glove
graft
graze
grease
grip
guard
handle
hold
hinge
hit
hold
homogenize
hook
hoop
huddle
hug
impale
implant
impregnate
index
insert
install
interlock
intermingle
intertwine
jam
join
knit
lace

laminate
lather
link
locate
lock
lodge
lure
macadamize
magnetize
manufacture
marry
mate
medicate
mend
merge
mix
moisturize
nail
nourish
pack
paddle
paint
panel
paper
paste
patrol
peg
pelt
penetrate
pin
pitch
plant
plaster
plug
poke
pour
precede
protect
pump
push
ratify

recruit	seal	stripe
rendezvous	seduce	support
rescue	seed	suture
reserve	sew	tack
resolve	share	tape
retain	shelter	tether
reunite	shield	thatch
rig	sniff	thread
rinse	splint	touch
root	stab	unite
rub	staple	weave
saddle	stitch	wire
salt	straddle	wrap
save	strap	zap
screw	strike	zip

Contradiction

abandon	cover	disarm
alienate	cross	disassemble
blast	cull	discard
blind	decline	disconnect
block	defrost	discontinue
blot	degenerate	discount
cancel	demolish	discredit
choke	denounce	discriminate
clash	depart	disembark
cloak	depolarize	disengage
clutter	deport	disentangle
coach	descend	dislocate
collide	desensitize	dislodge
compete	destruct	dismantle
complicate	detach	dismember
conceal	detain	disorder
condemn	deter	dispose
confiscate	detour	disqualify
confront	deviate	disassociate
confuse	dig	dissolve
congest	digest	distend
contrast	dilute	dive
convert	dip	divert
corrode	disable	divorce
corrupt	disapprove	dodge

eradicate
err
erupt
excavate
extract
fall
fight
flip
flunk
force
frisk
gamble
grate
halt
handicap
haunt
hypnotize
immobilize
injure
invert
irritate
jar
jaywalk
jeopardize
jerk
jolt
knockdown
knockout
lacerate
lubricate
lump
mangle
mow
needle
negate
neutralize
nocturnalize
obstruct
pinch
pivot
polarize
pollute

prod
punch
quit
ram
refund
refuse
regurgitate
reject
rejuvenate
repel
resign
resist
restrain
resurrect
resuscitate
return
reveal
reverse
revise
revoke
rupture
sabotage
salvage
segregate
separate
shade
shake
shock
singe
sink
skin
slam
smash
smear
snap
snare
sneak
sour
spoil
spy
squawk
squelch

stain
starch
steal
sting
stink
stir
strain
strip
suffocate
suppress
surprise
surrender
swagger
sway
swing
swivel
tangle
tarnish
tear
terminate
tranquilize
trick
twist
unbind
unbutton
unclasp
uncloak
uncover
uncurl
unglue
unhitch
unload
unlock
unpack
unravel
unreel
unscrew
until
unzip
veil
wreck
yield

Magnification

absorb
accent
accentuate
accomplish
accrue
accumulate
acquire
advance
advertise
alert
anoint
arm
assemble
astonish
attract
balloon
blitz
bundle
captivate
circle
circulate
climb
cluster
coagulate
collect
combine
complete
conceive
congregate
conjugate
connect
conserve
contain
converge
cook
couple
cross-pollinate
cultivate
cure
cup

cycle
defy
deploy
deposit
deputize
detonate
diffuse
dilate
distinct
document
double
dredge
dress
electrify
elevate
elucidate
emboss
emphasize
energize
enrich
erect
escalate
etch
evolve
exaggerate
excite
expand
explode
fatten
feature
ferret
fertilize
fill
finish
fly
focus
free
galvanize
garnish
generalize

generator
germinate
glaciate
globalize
gold-plate
goose
gorge
grow
harvest
hatch
hoard
hoist
identify
ignite
illuminate
immortalize
impress
imprint
include
increase
inflate
infuse
integrate
intensify
intoxicate
italicize
jack
jingle
jot
justify
jut
keep
kindle
kiss
knead
launch
lasso
leap
levitate
liberate

lift
log
magnify
manicure
maximize
metastasize
mobilize
monopolize
mount
multiply
nourish
objectify
obtain
occupy
open
operate
outgrow
outfit
outlast
outline
outwear
overcook
overheat
overstretch
overwind
oxidize
parade
pawn
perch
perpetuate
persist
play
please
point
pool
polish
post
preserve
print
project

prolong
propel
punctuate
quadruple
quantify
radiate
raise
rattle
reap
refresh
regain
register

reign
release
replenish
reproduce
retrieve
saturate
score
spot
sprawl
spread
spring

sprout
spur
stand
star
start
steep
stimulate
strengthen
stretch
swell
tabulate

tag
thicken
thrill
thump
toast
triple
upgrade
uplift
warm
whistle
widen

Miniaturization

abbreviate
ablaze
allocate
annihilate
aspirate
atomize
bleach
bore
bottle
bracket
brake
bridle
burn
calibrate
chew
chip
chisel
chop
classify
close
collapse
compress
condense
confine
constrict
cool

crack
cram
cramp
crease
cross-reference
crumble
curtail
cut
dampen
decode
decrease
deduct
define
denominate
denote
depict
deplete
depopulate
depress
deprive
detail
detect
devour
digitize
dim
diminish

disappear
disintegrate
dispense
dissect
dissipate
dissolve
distill
divest
divide
dot
drain
dribble
drip
enclose
engulf
evaporate
exfoliate
exterminate
extinguish
fate
fragment
frame
freeze
fry
gelatinize
grind

ground
half
hide
humiliate
hush
ice
imbricate
incase
isolate
knot
latch
limit
measure
miniaturize
molecularize
muffle
mute
muzzle
neglect
nibble
nix
nullify
obliterate
package
peel
pepper

piece
point
prune
pulverize
purge
quarter
raid
reduce
relinquish
restrict
rob

sack
saw
scale
scoop
scrub
sculpt
sever
sharpen
shave
shed
shall

silence
simmer
skin
slash
slice
splice
split
spray
sputter
squeeze
squish

submerge
summarize
surround
thin
tie
transistorize
trap
undercook
vaporize
wind

Simulation

activate
amend
appeal
appease
approximate
assert
assign
beam
bronze
budget
camouflage
capitalize
carve
cast
charge
choreograph
compare
compliment
comply
con
conform
conjure
contour
customize
dance
decorate
delegate
demonstrate
describe
direct

disguise
display
distort
dramatize
draw
dream
echo
embalm
endorse
engrave
equate
estimate
euphemize
exhibit
fabricate
forge
fossilize
glamorize
glide
graph
harmonize
heal
hitch
hybridize
idolize
illustrate
imitate
inbreed
incarnate
indemnify

ink
inlay
inscribe
joke
lubricate
match
mimeograph
mimic
mirror
model
oil
pace
parallel
pattern
personify
photograph
profile
qualify
quote
reciprocate
recite
refine
refinish
rehearse
reincarnate
reiterate
renew
renovate
repeat
replicate

reprint
resonate
restore
retrace
retread
revamp
review
revolve
select
shellac
snooze
spark
squeal
stage
stalk
stencil
synchronize
syndicate
synthesize
systematize
tail
tailgate
taste
tattoo
trace
track
translate
trowel
type
x-ray

Substitution

abbreviate
abduct
abort
abolish
amputate
arrest
audition
automate
bail
borrow
bypass
censure
code
delegate
deputize
displace
ditch
drop
dump
eclipse
eject
exchange
hibernate
ignore

incubate
indent
interchange
interject
interpolate
interrupt
intersect
intersperse
junk
lapse
lease
leave
legislate
lend
mechanize
mediate
obsolete
pawn
phone
pinch hit
punt
radio
raffle
reciprocate

recycle
redeem
reflect
relieve
remove
replace
retire
retool
sacrifice
scrap
skip
smoke
spare
substitute
succeed
supersede
suspend
swap
switch
symbolize
toss
trade
transpose
trim

EXHIBIT 27.

Evolving Showcase (95)

This brainwriting variation creates an atmosphere similar to a visit to a local art gallery. Based on the brainwriting techniques of Parnes, Noller, and Biondi (1977),[1] the Evolving Showcase, developed by Bil Holton, is designed to allow employees to browse among ideas (masterpieces) that have been recorded on flip chart paper to be placed on walls or flip chart stands. Employees involved in the ideation process are to add new ideas, jot down questions, record thoughts, and come and go as they please during the agreed upon time limit for the ideation session. The basic steps for this interesting (and productive) variation are

1. Flip charts on stands or chart paper pinned to designated wall space in a small conference room is organized to prompt ideas from team members. Each wall has a theme. For example, one wall would be posted with chart paper labeled "New Ideas." A second wall would post chart paper labeled "Questions." Another wall would display chart paper labeled "Serendipitous Thoughts." The idea is to prompt as many creative reactions as possible that are relevant to the problem. The fourth wall would display the problem statement and provide opportunities to record possible problem redefinitions. Variations would include listing different problem statements on each wall and asking for solutions, listing wishes for changes that would solve challenges facing the group, brainstorming about training needs, soliciting comments on the things the group does well, and so forth.

2. At the start of the day the ideation consultant leads a brief meeting to share the identified problem with the group and explains the steps involved in the Evolving Showcase process.

3. Members are encouraged to visit the gallery during the course of the workday and record their ideas, thoughts, redefinitions, and questions on the chart paper provided.

4. Several times during the day, the ideation consultant monitors the team's progress and encourages group members to contribute their ideas. Times are scheduled during the workday specifically to build in

[1] Parnes, S. J., R. B. Noller, and A. M. Biondi, *Guide to Creative Action*, rev. ed. (New York: Charles Scribner's Sons, 1977).

ideation opportunities. Employees are asked to visit the showcase area often to view the posted ideas and add their own.

5. Depending on the scope and criticality of the problem, the Evolving Showcase could remain open for several days or as long as a week.

6. When the number and quality of ideas generated seem sufficient, the team examines the ideas and selects those deserving further attention.

7. Appropriate Breakthrough Management® techniques are then employed as follow-ups to maximize ideation profitability.

EXHIBIT 28.

Visualization Bibliography (98)

Assogioli, R. *Psychosynthesis*. New York: Hobbs, Dorman & Co., 1965.

Bakan, P. "Imagery, Raw and Cooked: A Hemispheric Recipe." In *Imagery: Its Many Dimensions and Applications*, edited by J. E. Shorr, G. E. Sobel, P. Robin, and J. A. Connella. New York: Plenum, 1980.

Bry, Adelaide. *Visualization*. New York: Barnes & Noble Books, 1978.

Campbell, J. *Myths to Live By*. New York: Bantam Books, 1972.

Galton, F. *Inquiries into Human Faculty*. London: MacMillan, 1883.

Jacobson, E. *Progressive Relaxation*. Chicago, IL: University of Chicago Press, 1942.

Jung, C. G. *Collected Works*. Vol. 9, London: Routledge & Kegan, 1973.

King, S. *Imagineering for Health*. London: Theosophical Publishing, 1981.

Korn, E. R. *Visualization: Use of Imagery in the Health Profession*. Homewood, IL: Dow Jones-Irwin, 1983.

Krippner, S. *Galaxies of Life*. New York: Interface, 1973.

Kubie, L. "The Use of Induced Hypnagogic Reveries in the Recovery of Repressed Amnesiac Data." *Menninger Clinic Bulletin* 7 (1943): 172–183.

Leuner, H. "Guided Affective Imagery (GAI)." *American Journal of Psychotherapy* 23 (1969): 6.

Luria, A. *The Mind of a Mnemonist*. New York: Basic Books, Inc., 1968.

Luthe, W. *Autogenic Therapy*. New York: Grune & Stratton, 1969.

Mishra, R. *Yoga Sutras*. Garden City, NY: Anchor Press, 1973.

Richardson, A. *Mental Imagery*. New York: Springer Publishing Co., 1969.

Samuels, M., and H. Bennett. *The Well Body Book*. New York: Random House Bookworks, 1973.

Samuels, M., and N. Samuels. *Seeing With the Mind's Eye*. New York: Random House, 1975.

Sheikh, A. *Anthology of Imagery Techniques*. Milwaukee: American Imagery Institute, 1986.

Sheikh, A., and D. Pachuta. *Guided Imagery*. Milwaukee: American Imagery Institute, 1986.

Wolpe, J. *The Practice of Behavior Therapy*. New York: Pergamon Press, 1969.

EXHIBIT 29.

Constellations of Experience (100)

Cycles The ebb and flow of customers at a retail store; the ups and downs of the housing market; bird migrations each year; birth and demise of countries.

Distributions The large number of post–World War II babies; an aging work force; the number of women in management; the number of PhDs in any given area of the country.

Movements Smoke over an airplane wing in a wind tunnel; employees' fast track up the corporate ladder; escalation of professional sports figures' salaries.

Probabilities The Washington Redskins and Buffalo Bills usually win home games; by the year 2000 more than 50 percent of the American work force will be over 55 years old; a person smiled at will smile back.

Processes How to convert grapes into wine; how to convert eggs, green peppers, onions, and cheese into an omelet; how to manufacture personal computers or soap or shoes or toothpicks.

Proclivities People tend to repeat behavior they are rewarded for; shy people usually avoid eye contact; high-status people generally have carpeted, paneled, and windowed offices.

Sequence The steps you go through to start a lawn mower; the procedure used to call up a computer program; the order in which you dress yourself.

Shapes Cracks in dried mud usually form 120-degree angles; newborn babies and octogenarians have similar physiques.

Similarities Tornadoes and emptying water from a bathtub spiral alike; anthill communities resemble human cities.

Tendencies The influence of a movie star who appears on TV commercials has crested; smiles directed at someone else will be returned.

EXHIBIT 30.

Garbage Can Paraphernalia (101)

Tin Can   Pencil holder, paintbrush cleaner container, miniature barbell weights, toy telephones, nail and screw storage containers, furniture coasters, headlights for homemade soapbox car, decorative plant holder, stilts, binoculars

Paper Napkins   Miniature parachute, place mat, paper doll clothes, bandit's mask, coffee grounds filter, hair rollers, toy partition, tent for mice, artificial carnations, wedge to steady a rocking restaurant table

Styrofoam Egg Carton   Golf ball storage container, toy igloos, packing material, bracelet, tiny bowls, decorations for string partitions, contact lenses for a giant, sleep mask, eye patch, dome city for ants, shoulder pads

Foil   Book cover, space suit for a chipmunk, miniature satellite dish, thermos mug, metallic plate, toy hubcap, toy meteorite, miniature baseball or football, hinge, money clasp

Bottle   Toy telescope, flower vase, toy anchor, flute, rollers to move heavy objects, policeman's blackjack, chair legs, doorstop, earplugs for the Abominable Snowman, summer home for exhibitionist ants

Cereal Box   Magazine storage container, three-story house for spiders, high-top footwear, multitiered file cabinet, clothespin box, hat, boxing gloves, portable toilet for dogs, wastebasket, file folder

Grease   Lubricant for wagon wheels, hair cream, slippery surface for flea ice-skating rink, caulking for windows, deep-heating rub for trolls, tanning oil for marshmallows, temporary canvas for secret messages, device for melting snow and ice, pincushion, bedding for artificial flower arrangement

Management Skills and Related Prescription Inventory

In this section, Management Skills and Related Prescription Inventory, specific performance improvement skills for managerial growth are identified. Following each skill are the numbers of the prescriptions that help apply that skill to the real world. Because the performance improvement value for these prescriptions is multifold, many can be used for more than one skill.

Planning, Organizing, and Analytical Skills

Planning Strategically, 15, 16, 31, 90, 93, 94, 99

Planning Tactically, 15, 16, 31, 68, 90

Anticipating Problems and Investigating, 2, 5, 9, 15, 16, 18, 31, 40, 86, 93, 94

Evaluating Alternatives, Orchestrating Contingencies, 9, 15, 16, 31, 40, 93, 94

Applying Past Experience, 9, 14, 15, 17, 21, 40, 90

Handling Interruptions, Unplanned Events, 15, 67, 90

Using Sound Judgment, 3, 9, 15, 31, 40, 44, 86, 90

Examining, Reexamining Outmoded Assumptions, 2, 3, 5, 8, 15, 40, 45

Dealing with Complexity, 3, 5, 9, 15, 16, 40, 72, 90

Managing and Facilitating Meetings, 2, 5, 6, 9, 13, 25, 90

Seeing the Big Picture, 4, 5, 8, 9, 24, 31, 33, 49, 60, 68, 70, 72, 90, 91

Allocating Data and Equipment Resources, 9, 15, 90

Evaluating Alternatives, 9, 15, 16, 18, 31, 40, 93, 94

Assessing Probabilities and Possibilities, 3, 8, 9, 15, 18, 31, 40, 43, 60, 93, 94, 100

Estimating and Predicting Outcomes, 15, 31, 33, 40, 43, 90, 100

Communication Skills

Speaking Publicly, 53, 54, 55, 90

Giving and Receiving Feedback, 2, 3, 5, 6, 7, 9, 13, 14, 15, 16, 19, 24, 25, 26, 28, 29, 43, 48, 60, 70, 78, 90

Listening Attentively, 2, 3, 5, 9, 12, 14, 16, 19, 25, 29, 48, 60, 70, 73, 90

Preparing Written Materials, 6, 7, 9, 28, 31, 46, 49, 51, 52, 53, 60, 76, 87, 90

Using Correct Grammar, 5, 6, 7, 28, 31, 46, 52, 90

Presenting Technical Information, 9, 16, 29, 51, 52, 53, 90

Managing Disagreement and Resolving Conflict, 2, 5, 9, 15, 16, 22, 50, 70, 90

Building Rapport and Cooperation, 1, 2, 3, 6, 7, 9, 10, 11, 15, 19, 20, 26, 49, 58, 90

Mending Relationships, 15, 22, 77

Using Audiovisual Aids, 2, 5, 12, 54, 90

Networking and Alliance Building, 6, 11, 15, 16, 25, 29, 32, 90

Selling Ideas or Recommending, 6, 9, 15, 16, 29, 32, 90

Orienting New Employees, 13, 20, 27, 28, 29, 31, 90

Projecting a Professional Image, 7, 20, 28, 29, 35, 47, 90, 92

Aligning Nonverbal Gestures with Verbal, 2, 35, 47, 90

Criticizing and Correcting, 3, 13, 17, 23, 44, 47

Problem-Solving, Decision-Making, and Analytical Skills

Assessing Operational and Human Resource Needs, 2, 8, 9, 12, 13, 15, 16, 57, 60, 90

Identifying or Gathering Relevant Information, 2, 3, 5, 9, 15, 16, 18, 20, 28, 31, 40, 46, 72, 90, 93, 94

Management and Supervisory Skills

Clarifying Roles and Responsibilities, 2, 13, 15, 20, 90

Permitting Honest Mistakes, 9, 15, 16, 17, 21, 90

Demonstrating Decisiveness, 2, 5, 15, 16, 60, 90

Respecting Individual Differences, 5, 7, 11, 13, 15, 19, 20, 24, 29, 34, 50, 55, 90

Using Common Sense, 2, 9, 15, 16, 67, 90

Measuring Job Performance, 9, 44, 72, 90

Setting Measurable Goals, 2, 5, 9, 15, 31, 68, 90

Keeping Records, Documenting, 5, 9, 16, 18, 28, 38, 44, 46, 60, 90

Determining Appropriate Rewards, Incentives, 20, 90

Empowering People, 2, 3, 5, 7, 14, 15, 16, 20, 90

Celebrating Success, 1, 7, 10, 15, 90

Demonstrating Flexibility, Adaptability, 2, 3, 15, 16, 32, 60, 67, 90, 93

Assessing Risks, 17, 21, 31

Responding to Customer Expectations and Needs, 70, 71, 72, 73, 74, 75, 96

Assessing Personal Strengths and Areas for Improvement, 38, 41, 76, 77, 78, 80, 81, 82, 84, 87, 88, 90, 91, 92

Delegating: Matching Assignments with Performance Level, 15, 20, 65, 90

Ensuring Transfer of Training from Classroom to Line Operations, 8, 90

Leadership Skills

Modeling Leadership Excellence, 2, 19, 25, 26, 27, 28, 29, 35, 36, 38, 39, 41, 90

Shaping Values, Character Building, 2, 3, 6, 12, 15, 19, 20, 24, 29, 41, 48, 49, 90

Articulating Performance Expectations Clearly, 5, 31, 90

Managing Change, 9, 15, 45, 67, 90

Gaining Commitment, Galvanizing Support, 2, 3, 5, 6, 7, 9, 15, 16, 19, 20, 22, 32, 50, 60, 90

Taking Risks, Experimenting with New Ventures, 2, 15, 16, 17, 21, 33, 60, 90

Encouraging Involvement and Participation, 2, 3, 5, 6, 7, 9, 11, 12, 14, 15, 16, 19, 20, 23, 60, 65, 74, 90

Instilling Pride, Respect, Passion for Excellence, 2, 3, 6, 7, 10, 14, 15, 19, 20, 28, 90

Emphasizing Quality, Quality Assurance, 3, 5, 6, 13, 16, 20, 60, 90

Mediating, Negotiating, 2, 9, 15, 16, 22

Working within Budget, 16, 33, 90

Managing Multiple Priorities, Time Management, 9, 16, 44, 61, 62, 63, 64, 65, 66, 67, 68, 90

Establishing Direction, 9, 15, 25, 26, 28, 31, 44, 68, 72, 90

Restructuring, Reconceptualizing, 2, 9, 13, 16, 33, 44, 60, 67, 90

Cultivating Customer-Driven Organizational Climate, 3, 16, 19, 20, 29, 48, 49, 56, 60, 90

Hiring or Firing the Right People, 20, 65

Demonstrating Enthusiasm and Positive Attitude, 1, 2, 3, 6, 7, 15, 20, 60, 90

Mapping Customer Needs, 70, 71, 72, 73, 74, 75, 96

Fostering Innovation, 93, 94, 95, 96, 97, 98, 99, 100, 101

Communicating Organization's Mission, Preaching the Vision, 4, 5, 19, 20, 49, 72, 90

Initiative

Professional Competence

Team-building and Coaching Skills

Recommended Reading

Albrecht, K. *Organization Development*. Englewood Cliffs, NY: Prentice Hall, 1983.

Albrecht, K. *Service Within*. Homewood, IL: Dow Jones-Irwin, 1990.

Albrecht, Karl, and Ron Zemke. *Service America*. Homewood, IL: Dow Jones-Irwin, 1985.

Anastasi, Thomas E., Jr. *Listen! Techniques for Improving Communication Skills*. Boston, MA: CBI Publishing Co., Inc., 1982.

Argyris, Chris. "How Learning and Reasoning Processes Affect Organizational Change." In *Change in Organizations*, edited by Paul Goodman. San Francisco: Jossey-Bass, 1982.

Atwater, Eastwood. *I Hear You: Listening Skills to Make You a Better Manager*. Englewood Cliffs, NJ: Prentice-Hall, Inc., 1981.

Bandler, Richard, and John Grinder. *Frogs into Princes: Neuro Linguistic Programming*. Moab, UT: Real People Press, 1979.

Bates, Jefferson D. *Writing With Precision*. Washington, DC: Acropolis Books Ltd., 1978.

Bhide, Amar. "Hustle as Strategy." *Harvard Business Review*, Sept.–Oct. 1986.

Blake, Robert R., and Jane S. Mouton. *The New Managerial Grid*. Houston, TX: Gulf Publishing Co., 1964.

Carlzon, Jan. *Moments of Truth*. Cambridge, MA: Ballinger, 1987.

Carnegie, D. *How to Enjoy Your Life and Your Job*. New York: Pocket Books, 1962.

Carnegie, D. *How to Stop Worrying and Start Living*. New York: Simon & Schuster, 1944.

Cooper, J. *How to Get More Done in Less Time*. New York: Doubleday, 1971.

Cooper, Ken. *Bodybusiness*. New York: AMACOM, 1979.

Crawford, R. *The Technique of Creative Thinking*. New York: Hawthorn Books, Inc., 1954.

Crosby, Philip. *Quality Without Tears*. New York: McGraw-Hill, 1984.

DeBruicker, F., and Gregory Summe. "Make Sure Your Customers Keep Coming Back." *Harvard Business Review*, Jan.–Feb. 1985.

Donaldson, Les. *Conversational Magic*. West Nyack, NY: Parker Publishing Co., Inc., 1981.

Drucker, Peter. *The Frontiers of Management*. New York: Dutton Press, 1986.

Dyer, William G. *Team Building Issues and Alternatives*. Reading, MA: Addison-Wesley Publishing Co., 1977.

Edwards, Richard. *Contested Terrain: The Transformation of the Workplace in the Twentieth Century*. New York: Basic Books, 1979.

Foster, R. *Innovation: The Attacker's Advantage*. New York: Summit Books, 1986.

Goldberg, P. *The Intuitive Edge*. Boston: Geremy P. Tarcher, Inc., 1944.

Hewlett, William. *Invention of Opportunity: Matching Technology with Market Needs*. Palo Alta, CA: Hewlett-Packard Co., 1983.

Hubbard, R. *Self-Analysis*. Los Angeles: Bridge Publications, 1987.

James, William. *The Principles of Psychology*. Cambridge, MA: Harvard University Press, 1983.

Jung, C. *The Undiscovered Self* (translated by R. F. C. Hull). Boston: Atlantic Monthly Press, 1957.

Kanter, Rosabeth Moss. *The Change Masters*. New York: Simon & Schuster, 1983.

Keyes, K. *Handbook to Higher Consciousness*. Coos Bay, OR: Loveline Books, 1975.

Kouzes, J., and B. Posner. *The Leadership Challenge*. San Diego, CA: University Associates, 1989.

Kuhn, R. *Handbook for Creative and Innovative Managers*. New York: McGraw-Hill Book Co., 1988.

Labovitz, George H. "Want to Find Out What's Going On? Take a Walk." *Wall Street Journal* (20 December 1982).

Lakein, A. *How to Get Control of Your Time and Your Life*. New York: Peter Wyden Publisher, 1973.

Lawrence, Paul. *How to Deal with Resistance to Change*. Harvard Business Review, Jan.–Feb. 1969.

LeBoeuf, Michael. *How to Win Customers and Keep Them for Life*. New York: G. P. Putnams Sons, 1987.

LeBoeuf, Michael. *Imagineering*. New York: McGraw-Hill Book Co., 1982.

LeBoeuf, M. *The Greatest Management Principle in the World*. New York: Berkley Books, 1985.

LeBoeuf, Michael. *Working Smart.* New York: Warner Books, 1979.

Lee, J. *Hour Power.* Homewood, IL: Dow Jones-Irwin, 1980.

McGregor, D. *The Human Side of Enterprise.* New York: McGraw-Hill Book Co., 1960.

Mackenzie, Alec. *The Time Trap.* New York: McGraw Hill, 1972.

Maslow, Abraham. "A Theory of Human Motivation." *Readings in Managerial Psychology,* 3d ed., edited by Harold Leavitt, et al. Chicago: University of Chicago Press, 1980.

Maslow, Abraham. *The Farther Reaches of Human Nature.* Middlesex, England: Penguin Books, 1971.

Matteis, Richard. "The New Back Office Focuses on Customer Service." *Harvard Business Review,* Mar.–Apr. 1979.

Mitroff, Ian. "Teaching Corporate America to Think About Crisis Prevention." *Journal of Business Strategy,* Spring 1986.

Molloy, John. *Dress for Success.* New York: Warner Books, 1975.

Morrison, James H., and John J. O'Hearn. *Practical Transactional Analysis in Management.* Reading, MA: Addison-Wesley Publishing Co., 1977.

Naisbitt, John. *Megatrends.* New York: Warner Books, Inc., 1982.

Naisbitt, John, and Patricia Aburdene. *Reinventing the Corporation.* New York: Warner Books, 1985.

Normann, Richard. *Service Management: Strategy and Leadership in Service Businesses.* New York: John Wiley & Sons, 1984.

Orsburn, J., L. Moran, E. Musselwhite, and J. Zenger. *Self-Directed Work Teams: Business One.* Homewood, IL: Irwin, 1990.

Osborn, A. *Applied Imagination.* New York: Charles Scribner's Sons, 1957.

Osborn, A. *Wake Up Your Mind.* New York: Charles Scribner's Sons, 1952.

O'Toole, James. *Making America Work: Productivity and Responsibility.* New York: Continuum, 1981.

Ouchi, William. *Theory Z: How American Business Can Meet the Japanese Challenge.* Reading, MA: Addison-Wesley Publishing Co., 1981.

Parker, G. *Team Players and Teamwork.* San Francisco: Jossey-Bass, 1990.

Peters, Tom. *Thriving on Chaos.* New York: Alfred A. Knopf, 1987.

Peters, Tom, and Nancy Austin. *A Passion for Excellence.* New York: Random House, 1985.

Peters, Thomas J., and Robert H. Waterman. *In Search of Excellence.* New York: Harper and Row, 1982.

Pfeffer, Jeffrey. "Management as Symbolic Action: The Creation and

Maintenance of Organizational Paradigms." *Research in Organizational Behavior* 3 (1981).

Porter, Michael. *Competitive Advantage: Creating and Sustaining Superior Performance.* New York: Free Press, 1985.

Progoff, J. *Journal Workshop.* New York: Dialogue House Library, 1975.

Quinn, James, and Chris Gagnon. "Will Services Follow Manufacturing into Decline?" *Harvard Business Review.* New York: John Wiley & Sons, 1984.

Rogers, C. *On Becoming a Person.* Boston: Houghton-Mifflin Co., 1961.

Rothlisberger, Fritz, and William Dickson. *Management and the Worker: An Account of a Research Program Conducted by the Western Electric Company, Hawthorn Works.* Cambridge, MA: Harvard University Press, 1967.

Rowan, Roy. *The Initiative Manager.* Boston: Little, Brown Publishers, 1986.

Scott, D. *How to Put More Time in Your Life.* New York: Signet Books, 1980.

Sheehy, G. *Pathfinders.* New York: Bantam Books, 1982.

Stein, Barry, and Rosabeth Kanter. "Building the Parallel Organization: Toward Mechanisms for Permanent Quality of Work Life." *Journal of Applied Behavioral Science*, July 1980.

Wallas, G. *The Art of Thought.* New York: Harcourt, Brace & Co., 1926.

Walton, Richard. "Establishing & Maintaining High Commitment Work Systems." *The Organizational Life Cycle.* San Francisco: Jossey-Bass, 1980.

Waterman, R. *The Renewal Factor.* New York: Bantam Books, 1987.

Wertheimer, M. *Productive Thinking.* New York: Harper & Brothers, 1945.

Wriston, W. *Risk and Other Four Letter Words.* New York: Harper & Row, 1986.

Yuki, Gary A. *Leadership in Organizations.* Englewood Cliffs, NJ: Prentice-Hall, Inc., 1981.

Zemke, R. and D. Shael. *The Service Edge.* New York: New American Library, 1989.

Ziglar, Z. *See You At the Top.* Gretna, LA: Pelican Publishers, 1977.

Index